GODLESS HEATHENS

CONVERSATIONS WITH ATHEISTS

Edited by
ANDREW J. RAUSCH

Copyright © 2018 by Andrew J. Rausch

All Interviews by Andrew J. Rausch

Cover by Matthew Revert

All rights reserved.

No part of this book may be reproduced in any form or by any electronic or mechanical means, including information storage and retrieval systems, without written permission from the author, except for the use of brief quotations in a book review.

"I want to believe as many true things and as few false things as possible."

— Matt Dillahunty

CONTENTS

Introduction by AT TAYLOR	vii
JOE R. LANSDALE	1
MATT DILLAHUNTY	19
PZ MYERS	31
GREYDON SQUARE	45
AUTUMN CHRISTIAN	55
SHANNON LOW	63
DAN SAVAGE	73
ARON RA	83
MANDISA THOMAS	99
JOZEF K. RICHARDS	115
DAVE MCKEAN	123
PETE O'NEAL	133
JEN PEEPLES	147
SETH ANDREWS	157
KEITH LOWELL JENSEN	171
CASEYRENEE LOPEZ	181
GEORGE PERDIKIS	189
JIM CORNETTE	197
CHRIS ROY	209
About the Author	221
Also by CLASH Books	223
CLASH Books	225

INTRODUCTION BY AT TAYLOR

While the United States of America was founded as a secular nation after a revolt against religious tyranny, the overwhelming majority of Americans are not only raised as Christians, but many are also raised to believe that America is a "Christian nation." When so many of us are indoctrinated into these beliefs from the moment we are born, it can be a long journey and a painful battle to break away from the safety and support system one finds among like-minded people; but many of us are willing to potentially risk everything by coming out as atheists, because the truth is more important to us than pretending to believe just to remain in our comfort zones, or for the sake of others.

Deconversion from religion can be a long and painful process, fraught with family struggles and even being disowned by your parents. Admitting publicly that you no longer believe in the resurrection and miracles of Jesus or Christianity altogether can lead to unemployment, difficulties finding people to date and marry, and can even prevent people from running for public office.

For some popular atheist activists like Aron Ra and PZ Myers, there was an underlying skepticism of religion since childhood, while others were not raised in a particularly religious family. In these types of cases, it might be easier to come to the realization and admit to others that you don't believe in any particular religion, but the consequences of "coming out" as an atheist can still be disastrous.

Sometimes the road to losing one's religion takes a completely different path. Matt Dillahunty spent countless hours researching Christianity and other religions as he considered attending seminary, and was also concerned about "saving" his atheist roommate. This "backfired spectacularly," according to Dillahunty, and led to him becoming a non-believer. And as you might expect, his newfound disbelief also led to some conflict within his family at the time.

In any case, atheism is rarely, if ever, a rebellion against one's parents or a backlash against authority. We simply do not buy whatever religion is selling, and for many of us, a deeper investigation into various religions and the discovery of the many contradictions and scientifically false claims they make only serves to solidify our disbelief.

With the rise of the Internet and information more accessible now than ever, a seemingly endless library of articles, videos, and debates on religion are at nearly everyone's fingertips. Atheists and people who simply identify as non-religious are rapidly growing in numbers in America, and with that growth, even more atheist websites, YouTube channels, and activists are gaining ground and momentum as we keep fending off the same apologetics and arguments for Christianity that haven't changed much over the centuries. The atheist movement is growing stronger and stronger, much to the disapproval and frustration of some highly religious people.

We're beginning to see a strong backlash from religious

charlatans, fundamentalists, and evangelicals in America - many of whom approach atheist activism as some sort of doomsday or cult-like movement, when atheism is really nothing more than a lack of belief in religion and theistic claims. This backlash has largely exposed the dark underbelly of the highly religious, as much of their argumentation against religion relies on completely misstating the goals of non-believers (as if we aim to turn everyone into soulless devil worshipers), with many putting forth outright propaganda to demean and minimize the secular movement as a whole.

But unlike the pastors of many mega-churches and dishonest pushers of the "prosperity gospel," the secularism and atheism movements are not founded with the purpose of deceiving others for profit. We seek to live in a society where religious beliefs aren't used to discriminate or deny people of fundamental rights, and we want to feel as if our beliefs (or lack thereof) don't give us any particular societal advantage or disadvantage. In other words, we want everyone to be free to believe or not believe anything they like, so long as they're not using those beliefs to harm others or legislate what we do with our own bodies.

In this book, you'll hear the stories of atheist activists from a variety of backgrounds, including musicians, entertainers, educators, artists, writers, bloggers, podcasters, and YouTubers. Nearly all of them were devout believers at different points in their lives, but came to the realization that they could no longer hold on to those beliefs after examining them more closely. Many of these people have faced the negative consequences that can come with leaving your faith behind, along with the community of people you shared those beliefs with.

These are their stories, but we hope that some of you who are reading this can relate to their internal conflicts and social struggles, and perhaps feel better about your own "coming out" moment, or better deal with the consequences that may come when you admit to your loved ones how you really feel.

And to the believers out there reading this, we hope you might gain an understanding of how and why these people all left religion behind, despite the difficulty of doing so, and perhaps come to the realization that most atheists are just normal people like you that deserve to be treated with the same dignity and respect as everyone else—even if we don't share the same beliefs.

JOE R. LANSDALE

Popular author Joe R. Lansdale has written more than forty novels and thirty short story collections in a variety of genres, including Western, horror, suspense, crime, and science fiction. He has written chapbooks, comic book adaptations, and worked on *Batman: The Animated Series* (1992). Lansdale is perhaps best known for his offbeat Bram Stoker Award nominated novella *Bubba Ho-Tep* (1994). The novella, which depicts Elvis Presley and John F. Kennedy battling an undead mummy in a nursing home, was later adapted into a successful film by Don Coscarelli of *Phantasm* (1979) fame.

He is the author of the bestselling *Hap and Leonard* series, which (to date) includes nine novels, three novellas, and three short story collections. The crime series, which focuses on the exploits of best friends and private investigators Hap Collins and Leonard Pine, has also been adapted into the popular Sundance television series starring James Purefoy and Michael K. Williams.

Lansdale has won an impressive ten Bram Stoker Awards and has been nominated for another nine. He has received the

American Mystery Award, the Horror Critics Award, and the "Shot in the Dark" International Crime Writers Award. In 2011, he received the Bram Stoker Award for Lifetime Achievement and in 2012 he was inducted into the Texas Literary Hall of Fame. He has been nominated for the World Fantasy Award eleven times.

Lansdale continues to churn out books at the speed of light. In addition to his usual output of novels and short stories, he published the memoir *Miracles Ain't What They Used to Be* (2016). In the book's titular essay, Lansdale discusses his atheism and the many reasons he doesn't believe in gods. He calls God "the adult Santa Claus" and goes to work dissecting popular Christian apologist arguments. After reading this illuminating essay, I sought him out to talk with him about his beliefs.

In your interview with Terry Bison, "That's How You Kill a Squirrel," you said, "I actually am not against religion itself, but when people use it to justify bad behavior, or when they show how hypocritical they are, I always wonder if they've read the Bible they love to quote and shake." You've also said reading the Bible "cured me of Christianity." Isn't it strange how many Christians don't even know what's in the Bible? I find it both telling and funny that most atheists I know are far more knowledgable about the Bible than Christians are.

I think that's fairly common, because I think that's a lot of why we become nonbelievers. Actually reading it and seeing how similar it is to other mythology, and I think also that it's such a cultural element to our country that you would think people would be aware of it in the same way they are aware of *Huckleberry Finn* or something of that nature. That's what cured me. The more you read the more you see the obvious human failings in the construction and the inconsistencies and hypocrisy. I think what amazes me most is how many people I've met who claim to be Christians and haven't read the Bible, or they're misquoting it, or they're saying, "I know this because this is what my preacher tells me and he's called by God." As if I can accept that any more than accepting that my pitbull was called by God.

When people find out you're an atheist, a lot of them will say, "You just need to read the Bible. Have you read the Bible?" When you tell them that you are knowledgable of the Bible, it makes them uncomfortable and it kind of pisses them off.

It does. It's a step beyond that, too. It isn't just that a lot of atheists are well-read in the Bible, but they're often well-read in religion in general. I think a lot of times if you grow up in that and you have questions, you may even go to the Bible to reinforce what you think to be true, and then realize that it's not true. Then you begin to reinforce the other viewpoint of it being just part of mythology. I always thought that the fact that I grew up reading Greek and Roman and Norse mythology, and seeing those similarities sort of put me on that track and made me skeptical at first. Then by the time I was in high school I was a nonbeliever.

At what age did you let people know you were a nonbeliever, and what was the reaction to that?

It usually just came from asking questions. It wasn't so much saying "I'm a nonbeliever" as it was saying, "If that is true, then why...?" And then you keep getting answers like "he moves in mysterious ways," like a bowel movement. I just thought, well, that's not fulfilling. I never thought about calling myself an atheist or not an atheist, but it certainly was not a common viewpoint where I grew up. But I don't remember ever being afraid to say it, but I think I was about 18 when I was like, "You know what? I'm an atheist." [Laughs.] It was there before, but I think that's when I realized it in a concrete kind of way.

I think I tried to deny it for a long time. I tried to push those thoughts away. You're basically taught that to question these things is a sin in itself.

Oh, yeah. I did the same thing when I was younger. You know what I think is a unique point of view here is that when I was about eleven, I started out saying, "I'm gonna be a preacher." My mother was religious, but she was a skeptical religious person. And I don't think my father cared about it one way or the other. He told me, "Once you die, you're meat for the worms." But I don't think he would have ever thought of himself as an atheist; he just thought, "This doesn't make any sense to me."

I said, "If I'm going to be a preacher, I've got to know this Bible frontwards and forwards." Then I read it and I went, hmmm. So I started having questions, and then I started trying to make excuses for it, loopholes and denying this and that, but just as time went on... As I got older and started getting interested in anthropology, archaeology, and like I said I was already reading mythological texts or stories about Greek, Roman, and Norse mythology, and then later that expanded to others, then finally that's when I couldn't make any excuses for it anymore.

I'm not trying to be a dick, but I always thought it was funny that Christians would talk about other people's religions and mock them for being silly, but they don't seem to realize that their religion does a lot of those exact same things and handles things in the same manner as the ones they think are silly.

It's because they are culturally bonded. It's like when you grow up you can look at wherever you are born or raised, you can have some fairly accurate belief as to what that person's religious beliefs are gonna be. Not always, but... If you were born in a Muslim country, then you are very likely to be that religious ilk. Just like if you are born in certain areas you are more likely to be a Christian or a Jew or a Hindu or a Buddhist. That unto itself was one of my early suspicions that location had a lot to do with what you believed. That's what I think of and call cultural bonding. You bond with it to such an extent that you don't question it. I even saw something on TV the other day where they were listing these important historical events. "King David did this, and so and so did this..." But no one ever thinks to say, "That isn't history." But it's so built into our consciousness that we believe these people did these things. Sometimes you can't even find evidence that they exist. Of course even if you did find evidence that they exist, that doesn't make them part of a divine plan. Nor is there anything there that proves religion. But the starting point there is that they can't even find evidence that the Old Testament people existed, and for that matter Jesus is kind of a questionable thing too. He's mentioned maybe once in Josephus, and that's a suspicious mention, and I think he's mentioned like twice in some volumes that even the Christians doubt. You can't find mention of this incredible teacher anywhere else other than in the Bible or in this mention in Josephus which many people feel was sort of added in. And even then he's just mentioned in passing—he's not like this great guy. Then you start reading about Apolonius and Simon the Magician and you see how all those things have been conflated.

· · ·

One of the things you bring up in your essay, "Miracles Ain't What They Used to Be," is the Apocrypha, which most Christians don't even know exist. Why do you think so many Christians don't know about these deleted books of the Bible, and they did know about them, do you think they'd care?

It must make a difference to some since a lot of us started out in that religion as believers. The Apocrypha was one of the things that was also part of the dismantling of this cultural bonding. But I think for most people it wouldn't make a difference because they have made a commitment to a belief and they have built their entire lives around it. They have friends that go to church, they go to church, a lot of their life is involved with church. Even though a lot of people won't admit it, a lot of people that are heavy church-going people are more social Christians than they are theological Christians. That's often the case. I think they say there are about twenty percent they know of who are atheists, but that's just the twenty percent who are saying they are. There's probably a larger percentage in there that are atheist or agnostic and just aren't saying it.

I had a minister tell me one time, "Fake it till you make it. If you don't believe it, just pretend." I always thought that was really weird. That's common, but the Bible says God knows what's in your heart if he exists. So if you were faking it, it wouldn't get you anywhere. I always thought that was really bizarre.

I had a discussion not long ago; I forget how it came up. I don't go around pulling people's coat sleeves. But somebody brought it up to me. I don't care if you believe those things. I think you have the perfect right to. But somebody said, "You have to respect my belief." I said, "I respect your right to believe it. I don't respect your belief, or I would believe it." But the thing is, he said, "I just go ahead and decide to believe it because what if you're wrong?" I said, "Well, here's the problem with that," and it's the same thing you said. Biblically this powerful being is supposed to know what you are thinking and what you're believing, so that's just a false belief.

It does amaze me the degree to which people who are otherwise very intelligent and very discerning will just reject things that are common sense or just reject science out of hand and point at religion as being their reason why. I find that scary.

Yeah, I do too. When I was growing up in the Fifties and the Sixties there was heavy-ingrained religion and anti-Darwinism and all of that sort of stuff, but there was also a larger group of people who were willing to say "science is science" and religion was left to the church. There weren't these things that you put in school where they had religious doubts where they could come in and say, "Well, maybe Creationism exists." There was none of that. A lot of that had to do with John Kennedy when he came in and became president because he was very education and science-oriented, as was his wife. It They promoted that heavily. After World War II and the atomic bomb, that led people to become more aware of things that science knew and that science could do. Even comic books that I read—DC characters like Green Lantern and the Flash—promoted that. Prior to that, most of the characters had their powers through magic. But after World War II, they began to have powers through science because that was the big thing.

What I'm seeing now, you had those anti-Darwin and anti-science people in the Fifties and Sixties, and we're now seeing a growth of those people. They're ignorant and they're proud of it. It's the scariest damn thing, because when I was growing up there were people who thought we didn't go to the moon. Even my father, who was not an educated man and was in fact illiterate for all practical purposes, didn't believe we went to the moon. There was no convincing them. I'm thinking, 'so we spent millions of dollars to go out in the desert and fake it so they can tell us they did this.' And the Russians are in on it, too. It just becomes such a ludicrous thing. But if people can believe that, then they're gonna believe some guy died and came back and went to heaven and is waiting for you there. I was talking to someone and I said, "If God's all powerful, why didn't he just make everybody perfect to begin with?" They always say, "Perfection would become boring." I always say, "The actual definition of perfection is that it's perfect, therefore it could not become boring because it's perfect." I say, "Why are you trying to get to heaven? Is heaven perfect?" They say, "Of course." "So you believe perfection when it's time to, but you don't believe in perfection when it clashes with your basic mythology."

In your "Miracles" essay you bring up what has always been my favorite question about God, which is his apparent inability to cause severed limbs to grow back. This argument is usually a conversation stopper, as Christians have no real explanation for why their all-powerful God either cannot or chooses not to heal these people. Why, in the history of the world, did they never ever not even once grow back?

But at least in the Bible, if you're reading it, the people are cured of blindness immediately, and it's not like they have to go to the doctor and have medicine and recovery time. Somebody will say "Well, I died on the operating table." And I'll say, "Well, your body quit functioning for a while, but you obviously didn't die. You came back." They say, "It was a miracle."

"Well, how about all of those other people who died? What's so special about you?" Why is this happening? And if that is a miracle, why can't they grow back arms, and legs, and missing eyes? If their head gets blown off, why can't they just sew it back on there and pray and then they can get up and walk back home? Those are fucking miracles, and I don't want to hear about some goddamn birds singing in the tree being a miracle. It's miraculous in the broad term. We can all use that word, but it doesn't have to be theological; it can just mean amazing, or that it's surprising. Every day I think about the earth, or the universe, and the things they keep discovering, and to me, that is miraculous in one sense, but not what they mean in terms of God's miracles. In fact, if they go through those things immediately, they find they dug a hole too deep to get out, and by saying "Gee, there's all this miraculous wonderful stuff in the universe," it doesn't prove that there's a God in the universe. It proves a certain uniqueness and a wonder, and in a broader sense of nature and the cosmos, yeah, that's miraculous. But that has nothing to do with God.

People say "Well, how can you believe that just happened?" And I say "Well, I don't know how that's happened." But to ask me to believe in a science that I can't explain, these things that go on, doesn't really enforce the idea that there's a God, because in another way, you're asking me to believe, on some level, the same kind of thing—that there's a God always here, that there are these forces affecting nature and the cosmos. Now which one sounds the most logical? Some invented, supernatural deity who's been hanging around? They didn't have the better sense than to have to go on Zoloft at some point and to become more kind, and to decide that they're going to be Christians? Talk about a convoluted message and a convoluted way of doing it. The more that you look at it straight-eyed, the more ridiculous it seems. And that there's the one God, and you have all of this rigamarole. And from the beginning of time, you had a different plan, and yet, he's supposed to have an idea of how this all works. And what happened to all of these people before Jesus, if that's supposed to be the Christian's answer. What was their faith if they didn't know a Jesus because Jesus had not come down? You can just keep compounding these questions. And the answers are usually non-existent.

What'll happen nearly every time, if you keep asking these questions, is you'll feel them getting backed into a corner, and they'll say you have to take it on faith. And my take on that is and has always been that there are people in the world who have faith that the world is flat even in this day and age. There are people all over who have absolute faith in all kinds of other religions and ideas, so I don't have to take it on faith, and to me, that's just a "Get Out of Jail Free" card. That doesn't work for me. It's not an ultimate religion if it can't be obvious. If it's supposed to be an ultimate answer, why isn't it obvious?

In that essay you brought up a point that I've been making for years, and a lot of us have, that there's the situation with a guy in a trailer park who survives a tornado and 50 other people die but he claims he was saved by God. And then there's another example where there's a Bible—just the the book—survives a fire or an auto accident, in which human lives are taken, and then the saving of the Bible is said to be a miracle. I find that humorous and also sick that someone would think that a loving deity would place more importance on a book than on a human life.

They find His image in a cheese sandwich. "I can't explain babies with AIDS, but I'm gonna place Jesus's face in a fucking cheese sandwich, because that's really important." You know, if you believe in God, explain babies with AIDS. I hear some people say that they're being punished for what their parents did, and I say, "Your god punishes innocent children for what someone else did?" That makes no sense, at least in the way you're trying to tell me that your god is all-loving. You just have to accept that God's like what Twain said, that he's a maligned thug, or a malicious thug. Because that's exactly what you're telling me, but yet in the next breath, you're telling me that God is love and that all of these things are wonderful and what we need is more prayer. And every asshole who's got a mouth has been praying from the beginning of this religion for these things that never happen. If they want something and they get it, He answered their prayers. But God can't seem to figure out how to end wars, get rid of terrible diseases, abused children, abused animals; none of that stuff seems to be a priority for Him. It's more like if you pray for a car, and you get it, that's your prayer answered. And if you don't get it, it's God's will, meaning that He's never wrong. Prayer doesn't matter, because it just fits whatever you want to decide. It was either answered or it was God's will. It makes no sense. It's just conflicting testimony.

Nobody seems to take into account that prayer works approximately 50% of the time. It works in the same way that everything else works. Some shit happens and some shit doesn't. And they still say "Oh, it was the prayer." It's odd to me.

It's just another branch of things like numerology, astrology —they're actually all connected in some way, Even if a person does numerology or astrology, which is not religious, it's this idea that there's some organized purpose in the cosmos. I've had people tell me, "Well, my number is 9, and the person I married is number 9, and the date I got married is a 9..." And I say "Well, you know, if there's one true 10, counting the zero, you've got a lot of chances that that number is going to come up.

What if they don't come up? What does that mean? What it means is you're not identifying the times it doesn't come up. You're identifying the moments it does come up. And you're picking the moments it does come up that matter to you. But you can find a lot of moments where it did come up, but the moments didn't matter to you." It just doesn't mean anything.

You obviously say a lot of incendiary things about religion in your essay. When you sat down to write that, were you at all concerned about the likelihood that it might cost you some fans?

No. I can't live life like that. If people read my books, I think that it's pretty obvious that those elements are in my books. And I've often had Christians who were good people, and people say, "Why are the Christians always the bad people?" And I say, "If you read my work that close, you'll see that there are some good ones in there." A lot of my friends are Christians. And a lot of them live by the basic tenets like Jesus in the beatitudes. And if you live like that, I'm cool. But when you start using it as reasoning for hating gays or people of different religions, then I'm out. In the last 10 to 15 years of my life, I've actually lost a number of friends. Not because I'm an atheist, but because they're hypocrites, and they've grown to be stronger and stronger hypocrites, suddenly embracing ideas that they didn't embrace when they were younger. I don't know what's happened, but it's like there's a nut hole open, and all of these nuts are flowing through it. And it's not just religion. There have been a lot of people who are religious that I admire and respect. Jimmy Carter is one of my favorite Christians because he actually tries to do that stuff. And there are other people who try to do that stuff. And there are a lot of people who are social Christians who may not even think about the complications of it. But they go to church because it's part of their lives. I have some friends who say, "To tell you the truth, I don't think there's any afterlife, but I go to church because I really believe in those basic ideas of Jesus." And I get it. That's fine. The problem is that a lot of people in your group have a lot of different views on how to interpret those things. And my belief is that I can try to do those things and be a good person and a kind person without having to accept some mythical zombie.

In the essay you write, "Truth is, the gun-toting, tough-talking, warmongering Christians I know do not consider Jesus their hero so much as John Wayne. They don't want to turn the other cheek, they want to kill something. If it can't be a human, there's always a deer." I share those same views a lot of the time, and often find myself extremely leery of overly-religious people from the very start. If someone you've just met reveals themselves to be a Christian, do you find yourself guilty of immediate skepticism?

I'm skeptical in the same way that when I tell them I'm atheist, they're skeptical. But on the other hand, that doesn't mean that some of those people don't become good friends of mine. They have; at least associates or friends. But I'm always skeptical because religion is one of those things that always lets me down. With my good friends, they bring the better aspects of it. But you have people who start talking about Christianity and the next thing out of their mouth is something hideous about gays or black people or Hispanic people or you name it. And that's not to say that atheists can't be racist or be assholes, because they certainly can be. I know some people who are atheist that I wouldn't piss on them if they were on fire. I'm not trying to make this point that being an atheist makes you good. It doesn't, but it doesn't make you evil either. And some people have this idea that being an atheist is like being a Satan worshipper. They don't even know what it means, but they can't embrace it.

I don't often tell people I'm an atheist because I don't want to get into and argument about it, and they'll never change their minds.

But sometimes they do. I've seen some people in my life who changed their minds because of discussions that we've had. I wasn't out to change their minds. They were people who just start thinking about it and they say, "You know what? Yeah, where's the answer in this?"

At first, my next question is going to sound like it's unrelated, but it's not. It's actually very closely related. As an atheist progressive living in a red state, what are your thoughts on Donald Trump?

I loathe him. I can't stand the guy. And one of the reasons why I can't is the embracing of Christianity and that the Christians who voted for him are putting him on a pedestal and have decided that he can do no wrong, and they say they can forgive, but they can't forgive Hillary Clinton or whoever else they don't like. They can forgive the person who is a racist jackass and who is an anti-woman leader. I just don't get it; I don't understand it. I don't understand why they can't see their own hypocrisy. It's sort of like the water's up to their neck, and they think they're still on dry land. They just can't get that because most of the Christians I know, and I'm not saying this is all of them, are sadly in that camp. They're willing to let him do what he wants, be who he wants—they're willing to accept pussy-grabbing; they're willing to accept all of these things that he's done; they're willing to accept that he won't stand up for a woman; that he mocks people who are Muslim who have lost a son in our military, and so on and so on. The list is endless. I just can't figure it. I don't know what to think. I'm surprised he's lasted this long.

I knew he was going to be elected, though. Before the election, a couple of weeks out, I thought 'Oh my god. He's going to win.' Not because most people are going to vote for him, but because *enough* people are going to vote for him. I knew they were going to vote in areas where Democrats had decided not to really put their resources. And I remember when they were making fun of him for flying out to all of these little places at the last minute, and I thought that's where they were screwing up. Because it makes them seem elitist first of all. Second of all, these are vital areas to the electoral college. And they ignored them. I said I thought he was gonna win, and I had friends who were progressives who said I was crazy. They said, "Look at the polls." I'd say, "Yeah, look at them. They go up and down everyday, constantly. That means that there are a lot of people that just won't change; there are a lot of people who are lying when they won't admit they're voting for the pussy-grabber-in-chief." That was exactly what happened. So when it did, I wasn't surprised. I was shocked, even though I was right, but I wasn't surprised.

I do think a reckoning should be coming. I was pretty sure it was, but I've gotten to where I don't know anymore, because there's not a thing he can do that seems to have an impact on that hardcore thirty, thirty-five percent. And I hate to say this, but a lot of those people are just plain dedicated to trying to reproduce this America of the Fifties and Sixties that never really existed. What they mean is 'white.' I was talking to a friend of mine who voted for Trump, and I said, "How many people on the Democratic side belong to the KKK or belong to the Aryan Nation or belong to these Hitler-like organizations and came out in support of Clinton?" None. "But they do come out in support of you guys." He said, "He can't help who votes for him." I said, "Why do you think they voted for him? Why do you think he got their support and the other one didn't or there wasn't some kind of split support?" It's obvious what it's about.

Some of the people I know that I never really thought of as racist actually are, because they're telling me about how the white people are losing their power. I thought, you know what? Being white has never hurt me a bit, and I come from the poorest backgrounds, and I have known people who have come from equal or worse backgrounds, and I got opportunities they didn't get. I guarantee you it was their skin color. I just get tired of the horse shit. I remember one time my wife and I—this was in the Nineties—were in a restaurant and we heard some people talking. He said about Affirmative Action, "I wouldn't hire any of those you-know-whats if I didn't have to." That's when I thought, people keep telling me things are getting better, and they tell me Affirmative Action isn't needed, and then I hear people talking like that... And now we're seeing the results of all that. These guys are coming in and saying, "We don't want to give any special privileges to those people." I certainly believe as soon as we get to the point where people are hired on the basis of their character and their skills and not their color, we can get rid of that. And maybe we're closer to that than we once were, but man, what Trump did, and actually what Obama did as far as people reacting to him being a Black President, it's all revealed this nasty, deep divide where people are showing what they really believe. It's scary and it's sad.

. . .

I think it's frightening that polls repeatedly show that Americans would rather have a pedophile be President than an atheist.

It's crazy. I've had this happen numerous times when people found out I was an atheist. "God, I thought you were a Christian." I say, "Why did you think that?" They say, "Because of the way you act and the way you treat people." I thought, in other words I'm not doing it for a reward—I don't get to go to heaven and play a harp like I want to—but I'm doing it because I think it's the right thing to do. I'm setting a positive example and being a positive force in the universe. If you want to do something that is a force, it's your actions and how they're passed on. Don't get me wrong, I'm not trying to paint myself as some perfect person. I am not. But I've done the best I can, and certainly I've made the right and proper effort.

MATT DILLAHUNTY

Matt Dillahunty was raised in a Southern Baptist family and was, for many years, a devout Christian. After serving eight years in the Navy, he felt he was compelled by God to become a minister, leading him to study and investigate the Bible (and other related subjects) more closely. These studies ultimately led him down a path to atheism. "After the first couple of years, reason forced me to acknowledge that my faith had not only been weakened by my studies—it had been utterly destroyed," he has said. "The thoughts, writings, and wisdom of people like Robert Ingersoll, Voltaire, Dan Barker, Richard Dawkins, Farrell Till, and many others, helped free my mind from the shackles of religion without a single moment of despair."

Since that time, Dillahunty has become one of the loudest and most recognizable voices in American atheist activism. He has hosted the webcast cable-access television program *The Atheist Experience* since 2005. He was the president of the Atheist Community of Austin from 2006 to 2013. He was the host of the live Internet radio show *Non-Prophets Radio*, and is a founder and contributor of the counter-apologetics encyclopedia, *Iron Chariot*. He travels the world speaking as part of the Secular Student Alliance. He frequently debates noted Christian apologists. He and fellow atheists Seth Andrews and Aron Ra, known collectively as "the Unholy Trinity," traveled to Australia to speak in 2015. He has also been invited to speak at the Merseyside Skeptics Society QED Con in the United Kingdom.

* * *

At one point you attended seminary and studied to be a minister. You've said that your road to atheism began with your seeking to learn how best to witness to atheists. Would you like to talk about that?

I never attended seminary. That gets passed around all over the place online. I think it even popped up on Wikipedia at one point. I had intentions of going to seminary at one point, but I found my way out of religion prior to that. My roommate at the time was an atheist. I had spent eight years in the military and had then worked in the tech industry, and as a teenager there were people in my family and in my church who were convinced that God wanted me to be a minister. I was terrified of public speaking, so I didn't want to be a preacher. And then after being in the Navy and working in the tech industry and losing my job, I thought God was punishing me. I thought God was saying, "Hey, I called you to the ministry. You decided to focus on your career, and now I'm going to take all that away." So I got serious and spent about a year-and-a-half or so in pretty serious prayer and study.

Because my roommate was an atheist and we were best friends, I didn't want to get right with God, die, and go up to heaven and have God say, "Why is this guy, whom you love like a brother, burning in hell because you refused to share the gospel with him?" I set out to try to find the best ways to communicate the gospel with someone who was an atheist. I had a lot of confusion about this, because growing up steeped in religion and surrounded by everyone who believed similarly to me, I'd certainly met and witnessed to a lot of atheists. I just hadn't known enough to recognize that they were atheists. In my mindset at the time as a believer, they were people who didn't believe. But they weren't atheists. Atheists were rabid God-hating, God-denying people. So it was fundamentally different to talk to someone who just didn't believe. I came to realize that they are atheists. My trying to find the best ways to have the conversation with him ended up backfiring rather spectacularly, and I ended up a nonbeliever.

There's a misconception that many Christians have, and I certainly had it when I was a Christian. It's that atheists are people who start out as Christians who are angry with God for some reason. It's like that misconception that people in porn films were abused as children. Everyone's path in life is different, and there's no one overall explanation that covers everybody. Why do you think they believe that? Another misconception is that we worship the devil. Why are these misconceptions so prevalent?

I think a lot of it is the fact that religion has had a somewhat unfair advantage. Everything that people know about atheists, up until the popularity of the Internet, probably came from their preachers and the other believers around them. So you kind of build atheists up into this myth. Most people probably thought of Madalyn O'Hair, and that was probably their only knowledge about atheists.

Another aspect is that we're all convinced that we're right.

If we didn't think we were right, we would change our minds, change our positions. So if you are a believer, and I guess I can primarily stick with Christianity, because it's what I grew up with and it's popular in the United States, if you think you're the true religion, God loves you, and everything else... Christianity is one of the religions that has the correct defense mechanisms to have survived this long. Basically when religions make claims that are easily debunked, they fall by the wayside. When you have this idea that you have the truth and you have a God who cares about you, when you've made a public profession of your faith...all of those things work together to set it up so that you can't possibly be wrong.

One of my biggest pet peeves, and this came up in a debate I did in Canada. It was myself and Chris DiCarlo against two ministers. He made the assertion that we've all heard over and over again, which is, "If you would just open up your heart to God he would reveal himself to you." And when you try to say you have in fact done this, their response is, "No, you haven't. There's something wrong with your heart, there's something wrong with the way you did it..." The issue here is that they set something up where they can't be wrong, because if you open yourself up to God and he doesn't answer, then it's your fault. There's something fundamentally wrong with you. They've set up an unfalsifiable position, a no-lose situation essentially. It makes them more comfortable in dealing with that situation, because if they had to admit that I sincerely, in all correct fashions, reached out to God and got no response, then they would have to acknowledge they were wrong and everything begins to crumble after that.

When you first came out as an atheist, how was this news met by your friends and family?

It was pretty strange, because I was actually hosting the TV show before I had come out to any of my relatives. I was planning on potentially writing a book that would make the subject accessible, particularly to my parents. I was trying to figure out the best way to have the conversation. I was actually outed by an uncle. What ended up happening was, it caused a rift. My relationship with my parents is fine today, even though they're still convinced that I'm working for Satan. But it was a really difficult time because my dad told me I couldn't love anybody, because God is love and without God in my life it was impossible for me to love anybody. So if I tried to end the phone call with, "I love you, Dad," it was kind of "no, you can't. But I love you." There was a lot of this using religious belief as a weapon, as a form of attack, because they were on the defense. What ended up happening is that it became very difficult to reconcile the fact that here is your child whom you know is a good person and whom you observe doing good things, whom you love, and yet the God you desperately hope is real and are convinced is true is telling you—or the religion is telling you—that this individual is not only lost and deserving of hell, but is someone you shouldn't interact with. So things will never return to the old normal, but we've established kind of a new normal. My wife had far more difficulty with some of her relatives, but that sorted itself out after about 20 years.

I'm more worried about young people that I hear from who acknowledge their atheism and are then thrown out by their parents. I've had to help relocate a couple of different people and find places for them to live because of that. I think in the Internet video that everybody kind of laughs at where the kid says he's an atheist and then the initial reaction is "no Christmas presents for you," it's clear that they're desperate to say something but they don't know how to deal with it. When I called and told my dad, he said something along the lines of,

"Okay, I'm going to have to think about this," and then hung up. What I've since found out that the did was he went to Wikipedia and looked up "atheist." Then shortly thereafter he and my mom went to a Lee Strobel event to talk to Lee. "Hey, our son's an atheist. What should we do?" And Lee just sold them a couple of his books. Last year when I finally had a chance to meet Lee I told him that story and suggested that he stop just shoveling his books to parents and actually tell them to talk to their kids.

When you tell someone you're an atheist, they take that as a personal attack on their beliefs. We don't feel that way. Unless you're pushing your beliefs onto me, I don't feel attacked by the fact that you believe in Jesus. Why do you think Christians take it as a personal affront if we don't believe what they believe?

I think it's two things. One is that it's been drilled into them in one form or another that atheists are in opposition to Christ and religion, and therefore you're immediately viewed as dangerous and the enemy. The second factor is, and I don't want to pretend I can read people's minds, but I know that believers constantly struggle with doubt, otherwise there wouldn't be apologetics and all of these discussions wouldn't occur. I think the knee-jerk fear reaction is a resignation to some cognitive dissonance. On some level they have to realize it could easily be viewed as preposterous. And if they entertain the notion long enough, or seriously enough, they might lose their belief, which is something they desperately don't want to happen.

You've become famous for your debates with Christian apologists. You've had a lot of them. When you go into a debate like that, personally for you, what is your primary goal? What do you hope to accomplish when you enter into that debate?

I'm not trying to change my opponent's mind, but I am trying to reach people in the audience who may watch. Two goals for me are that I need to keep in mind that this is probably going to be somebody's initial introduction to secularism, atheism, humanism, skepticism; they have never encountered this before. Part of that is making sure I'm the best representative I can be. The other goal is to make sure the discussion is as honest as possible. If it turns there is a God, I'd like to know. If it turns out that all I'm going to be offered is anecdotes and fallacies and absurdities, then I think there's a responsibility to point those out as honestly and forthrightly as possible. Debate is quite often theater, where you might actually have the best arguments and the other person, through their personality or whatever, connects more, and the facts can get overlooked. I'm trying to push away from structured debates and move more towards discussions, because I trust audience members to be able to look at this and tell who's thinking and who has spent time thinking about this and who is regurgitating someone else's thoughts and stock lines, and who is actually responding to what their opponent is saying and asking for clarification and trying to get to some level of understanding, and who is just there to preach.

Most of us aren't as skilled or as experienced as you are at having these debates with Christian apologists, but they do come up from time to time. In your mind, what are some things you think a person should recognize or be aware of when going into such a debate?

There are a couple of talks I've given on this, and I'm not going to remember all of them today, but I would say going into it with the right motivation is key. If you're just going in to show how smart you are or make fun of the opposition or to mock, then that's probably not the best course of action. You should always acknowledge that you may in fact be wrong. You should be honest. I hate bad arguments, but I hate them most when they come from people who are defending positions that I think are reasonable. I end up arguing and fighting with atheists as much as anybody. I think the key is to actually put the burden of proof where it should rest. If someone is claiming something supernatural—that there's a God or an afterlife—they have a burden of proof. It's not up to you to prove them wrong. That may in fact be impossible, because they could have an unfalsifiable position at their disposal. What I see many people doing is, in order to push back even harder, they begin to engage in hyperbole that puts them in the position where they have the burden of proof rather than just saying, "You claim there is a God. Please provide your case for this," and then pointing out how they haven't met the burden of proof. Some people might respond, "There are no gods." You may be able to demonstrate that. It depends on definitions. But I think it's a mistake to do that unless you are confident you can meet that burden of proof. Because if you fail to meet that burden of proof, in the minds of many, the other side wins. You've switched where the default position is. It should be, "I do not and will not believe that a God exists until such time that it has been demonstrated."

In the countless debates you've had, you've had stuff thrown at you in varying degrees of quality. What stands out in your mind as being some of the more ridiculous statements or arguments?

I think one of the strangest ones was actually when I was debating the issue of whether or not Jesus rose from the dead.

My opponent started by saying there were two lines of evidence. The first was to show that reality has a supernatural component to it, and the second line was to share that the historical evidence shows that Jesus rose from the dead. Only the second line of evidence is relevant to the debate. The first line is an attempt to poison the well, because if you get people to believe in the supernatural, then all of a sudden there's a proposed explanation surrounding everything you're trying to prop up later on. But in the first part where he's trying to argue for the supernatural component, he's telling stories about Ouija boards and trash can lids flying and a church praying for a certain amount of money and then that amount of money arrives. This is all demonstration of seriously flawed epistemology—a failure to understand and apply skepticism and critical thinking. I'm happy to believe that somebody has had an experience that they do not have an explanation for, but when you assert that you do—the trash can lid moved and it was because of a ghost—you need to actually demonstrate that. You don't get to just say, "I can't think of any better explanation." That's how we've gotten into all of this. "I can't think of a better explanation."

I know you've personally been responsible for changing some people's outlooks on religion or sending them down a path towards atheism. What is it like to know that you've reached those people, and has that happened frequently?

It happens all the time. I get thousands of e-mails and I've been hosting the TV show for thirteen years. I was in Chicago for an event with Sam Harris Saturday night and there were just shy of 3,000 people. I met a couple dozen or more people who wanted to thank me for helping them escape from religion and become a skeptic or a humanist or whatever. My answer for all of them is, I like that this has happened because it's always good to know that your efforts and the time that you've put into something has been helpful to people. But I also tell them, "Don't give me credit for changing your mind. You changed your mind. There were a thousand other people who heard me say the same thing, and they didn't change their minds. So own the fact that you were willing to follow the facts wherever they led you, that you were willing to acknowledge the fact that you might be wrong and were open to changing your mind. I'm just a guy who talks a lot, but you're the one who did all the work." It doesn't quite play out like that because clearly I don't completely suck at what I do, and people have found that useful. I'm thrilled when that happens. But I also want people to acknowledge that they're the ones who did the hard work, and they were the ones who were open to changing. There are so many others who seem to be immune to reasonable discussion.

On the opposite side of that, regarding feedback, do you receive much negative feedback? Do you receive hate mail?

I don't get much hate mail. It's actually been pretty rare over the years. I get tons of e-mails, and certainly there are some people who are occasionally contentious, but not much of that. There have been a handful of threats over the years and a handful of really hateful messages. Largely I ignore them. There have been a couple threats that I've shown the authorities, but I've always said I was more worried about those people themselves. The people who are potentially dangerous probably aren't going to e-mail or call and tell you about how they're going to kick your butt. There's not much I can do about it. I guess I've been lucky in the sense that I haven't had to be too concerned with that. There are certainly some tenacious individuals who will e-mail repeatedly. I have received some e-mails from people who are clearly mentally disturbed in some fashion, but as I'm not a mental health expert I don't try to diagnose them and I don't try to interact with them. Their e-mails are incredibly disjointed and scattered. I've probably got 13,000 unanswered e-mails right now, so it's really easy for me to just focus on the conversations I have a good reason to think are going to be somewhat productive.

Recently you've been on a speaking tour with Sam Harris, Richard Dawkins, and Lawrence Krauss. What's it like working with those guys?
It's a little different every time. Richard and I met many years ago, and having private conversations with someone or just interacting at the same convention is a little bit different from trying to speak together onstage. You've got to build up a little bit of a rapport and find out what conversations each one likes. The first event that Sam and I did together was also with Richard in London. Sam and I had only met once before, for like a minute. There was no reason for him to have remembered that at all. The London event wasn't a bad event—I think most people liked it—but we didn't know enough about each other to really have a good conversation. I think that improved a lot in New York, and then we did Chicago last week. I took more of a backseat. I was specifically offering up questions in more of a host role, even though I know I'm not a host. I'm there to contribute as much as to control the flow of traffic, but Sam is incredibly popular. So when you have a 3,600-seat theater I know the bulk of the people there want to hear what Sam has to say. But I'm never going to put myself in a position where I'm nearly interviewing someone because I have things to contribute as well. I think we've gotten to the point where

everybody is comfortable with everybody and we can have a good conversation and I can sit back and be quieter on occasion or I can jump in. Lawrence likes to go toe-to-toe with either one of us. We had a 30-minute discussion on free will, and both Lawrence and I have taken Sam to task on some of his ideas.

As we talked about in Chicago, one of the reasons I didn't want to become a preacher was because I had a fear of public speaking. That's ironic now because it's completely vanished. I think the biggest reason for me is that if you're not trying to B.S. anybody or try to pretend that you know things you don't know and you're not overly-concerned about people's opinions of you, if you're honest about who you are, I've found that fear of public speaking has just vanished. You either like me or you don't, you either agree with me or you don't. We can have a conversation or we can't, but I can't change that. So I've really enjoyed these events and getting to know Richard and Sam and Lawrence more. There will be a couple more of these events together and then I sort of start out on a solo world tour with a magic and skepticism show.

PZ MYERS

PZ Myers is a professor of biology at the University of Minnesota, Morris, and one of the loudest voices in atheism today. He is an outspoken critic of Creationism and intelligent design. He writes and publishes the web blog *Pharyngula*, which is one of the top-rated scientific blogs on the Internet. Myers, a self-proclaimed "godless liberal," is also a huge proponent of the feminist movement.

In 2008 Myers drew international ire when, as a reaction to a controversy involving the Catholic church's treatment of a young man who had stolen a communion wafer from church, he encouraged readers of his blog to send him communion wafers and he would then treat the wafers with "profound disrespect and heinous cracker abuse, all photographed and presented here on the web." Upon receiving these wafers, Myers then went to work piercing the "goddamn crackers" with a rusty nail that had previously pierced copies of *The Koran* and Richard Dawkins' *The God Delusion*. For this "crime" Myers received tremendous backlash which included calls for him to be fired from teaching and even death threats.

The following year Myers made more waves when he took more than three hundred atheists to visit the Creation Museum in Petersburg, Kentucky, where many of them reportedly laughed and mocked the exhibits.

In 2009, he was named the American Humanist Association's Humanist of the Year. Myers is also the author of the Random House book *The Happy Atheist*.

* * *

Let's talk a little bit about your background in terms of religion. Do you have a religious history?

Oh, that's complicated. I was brought up Lutheran, but it never really took. I was a regular churchgoer as a child but the thing is, it was more of a social event. I really didn't believe, so I can't say that I was honestly ever at all religious.

You label yourself as a "godless liberal," which is a tag I can definitely relate to. Would you talk a little bit about how you see yourself?

My family went to church, but they weren't very devout, and it was more of a liberal tolerance and the liberal idea that you could better yourself. My father was big into unions, and the labor movement, like many people in the Pacific Northwest. It was just part of my foundation, this progressive liberal attitude towards the world.

What are some of your goals for your Pharyngula weblog?

I guess just keep it going. We entered a new phase just a few years ago because, well, to give you a little history, I was on Science Blogs for a long time. And then Science Blogs started having some difficulties. There were some ethical concerns that came up. They were clearly losing interest in maintaining a blog network. It's still there, and I've still got a presence there, but it's not a big deal. Ed Braden—another blogger there—and I decided that we wanted to establish our own network; let's start our own, let's do it for ourselves, and the goal of that network was to give a voice to people other than the usual atheists. You know how most of the famous atheists are white men, and we said that's not an appropriate representation of the way atheism is going so we really wanted to give a voice to other people as well.

So right now I have my blog. It's still there, but it's just part of a network where we regularly try to bring in new voices and give them blog space and have them writing alongside all of us.

One of the things you talk a lot about is the separation of church and state. As we're sort of moving away from that in this country, I wondered if you wanted to talk a little bit about that as far as what hope, if any, you see for the future?

After this last election, you ask me that? [Laughs.] I'm not very hopeful at all for anything there. I'm looking at the people that Trump is bringing into his administration and it's just a disaster all around. I have no idea who he is going to nominate for the Supreme Court, but that's going to be another catastrophe for separation of church and state. So, this is a major concern. I don't have much hope for the near future.

My only real hope is that there will be such a strong reaction against this that it will discredit the Republicans for many years to come and will get a big change coming in the next election. But then I've been saying that since Reagan, and I've been wrong all along, so who knows what will happen next?

. . .

Have you ever considered getting into politics yourself?

Well, I once volunteered to run for school board. I really think it's a good idea to start at those low-level, local positions, and I was strongly discouraged because I have a reputation, you may have noticed, as a noisy atheist, an obnoxious atheist, and it was felt that there was no way I would win in a fairly conservative area. I live in a rural part of Minnesota, so I don't think I have much of a chance.

As a "noisy atheist," what kinds of mail do you receive? What does your mail look like?

Regularly, lots of hate mail. Unfortunately, a lot of it is from atheists these days. That's been an unfortunate change. If you talked to me five, ten years ago, most hate mail was coming from Christians. But what's happened is the atheist movement has splintered a bit and there's a very vocal, very loud contingent now that is more concerned with slapping down feminism and equality and all that good stuff that progressive liberal atheists are all in favor of.

What do you see as a misconception about yourself?

I don't know. I mean, like you said, I get a lot of hate mail. Those people are all wrong about me, but in some ways they're right because they like to hate the things I actually stand for. But I think I've been pretty open and straightforward about myself. I mean I happily admit that I'm kind of abrasive and aggressive and very opinionated. When people tell me I'm those things, I just say, "Yeah, you're right."

. . .

What do you see as being the biggest misconceptions about atheism?

There are so many. I would put them in two categories. One category is misconceptions about atheism from people who are not atheists, and there you get a lot of misconceptions like atheism is like just another religion, or worse, that we're Satan worshipers or something absurd like that, and those people I don't think are much worth talking to. They're pretty much out of it. The other misconception that bothers me a great deal more is that within atheism there's a lot of people who think that atheism is nothing except disbelief in god that nothing else follows, that there's nothing that builds up to that; it's just a flat conclusion and we're done and anybody who tries to suggest anything more is totally wrong and is a danger to the atheist movement.

So that's actually the biggest misconception that bothers me a great deal because we all bring a whole bunch of baggage into atheism and sometimes people think that the absence of baggage means that they are purely apolitical, and no, that's not true. Everyone has these loaded ideas behind their beliefs.

You've obviously got some problems with intelligent design. What are some of your biggest beefs with intelligent design?

Oh, there are so many! Probably the biggest problem I have with intelligent design right now is this default assumption that being complicated is that it to have been designed. That's the root of most intelligent design claims. "Hey, if we just catalog all these things and it gets really complicated and really difficult and there are things we don't understand it means that the only way it could have happened is if a designer did it." And, of course, exactly the opposite is true. I would be more impressed if things were simple and elegant. That would be the hallmark of a designer. And when you get deep into biology, you discover that no, nothing is simple and elegant; it's all pretty complicated. And that does not say that there had to have been a god behind it. It says it's driven by chance processes, with a lot of accidental results and cobbled together bits and pieces. It's a result of tinkering rather than design.

Keeping religion out of science education is an issue that is very important to you. I wondered if you wanted to talk a little bit about that?

The future is looking grim. Today is the day that Betsy DeVos is getting grilled by the Senate. Well, I shouldn't say grilled, because she'll get likely roasted and accepted, I expect. She's basically a theocrat who wants to destroy the public schools and make for a more godly educational system. And so that's looking bad for the future.

As far as what I object to by inserting religion into the classroom is that religion doesn't answer anything. I'm teaching science and what we care about is what's the evidence, what's the facts, what's the logic behind your claims. Can you back them up? Can you test them? All that kind of stuff, and god belief is just short-circuiting that. It says no, forget all that; we're going to accept the divine word of this religious authority as the truth. And so it's literally anti-scientific to bring religion into the science classroom.

In 2007, you were one of a few people who got duped by filmmaker Mark Mathis for his Expelled: No Intelligence Allowed *documentary. Would you like to talk about that?*

Is it fair to say that I was duped? I mean, it became really obvious fairly quickly what it was all about, and I was just willing to go along with it. He contacted me and basically there were a whole bunch of lies behind it. Before I accepted the invitation to be interviewed, I checked into the background of this company, and there was a whole bunch of stuff on the Internet. There were all these lists of projects completed and projects proposed and these documentaries I'd never heard of, but that they claimed they had made. They had completely cobbled together a past for this company that had just sprung into existence for this one film, so that was sneaky. They got me, they got Eugenie Scott, they got Richard Dawkins, because we had all just said, "Look, okay, that's fine." We had no commitment one-way or the other to the purpose of the movie but we were willing to do an interview.

They had crews that went out to England to interview Richard Dawkins. They actually came out to Morris, Minnesota, where I live, which kind of impressed me. So they had some money behind the whole thing. But when they were here, it was all gotcha interviews. They were trying to catch me in something and it wasn't clear exactly what. And if you watch the movie, you'll notice that they didn't really catch me in anything because I think the most shocking thing I said was I expected that religion would someday fade away. I think they were hoping to catch me talking about marching people into death camps or something. With Richard Dawkins it was the same thing. They got these fairly innocuous comments that they had to bloat up with footage of goose-stepping Nazis and so forth in order to make it seem like we were saying horrible things.

Who are some of your contemporary atheist activists that you're most impressed with?

Who am I impressed with? The last couple of years have

been a lesson in not having any heroes, so I tend to criticize everyone. [Laughs.] But let's see, who do I think is really good? Dan Barker and Annie Laurie Gaylor at Freedom From Religion Foundation. I think they've been doing a really good job and they haven't been downplaying some of the social justice issues that some of the other organizations have been doing. So I kind of like them.

Matt Dillahunty is a really good guy who is really strong on debating and argument, so I really enjoy listening to him. Who else do I like? No, I don't like anyone. [Laughs again.] Everyone has their strengths and weakness. I like Neil DeGrasse Tyson for science, although I think sometimes he gets cocky. I like Bill Nye because he's got the touch; he can really get people connected to the science part. I like that about him.

On the flip side of that coin, I'm going to name a name and I'd like your thoughts on this person—Ken Ham.

He's a confidence man. I think he's sincere in his beliefs. I tend to think that when people say they believe something, they are actually being honest about what they believe. But he is so incredibly dishonest in his presentation of the science. It drives me nuts. He's also repetitive and not very well informed, so every time Ken Ham talks about science it's to present this bizarre economy of historical and observational science which is absolutely false. It has nothing to do with how people think about science at all. He's distorted a couple of terms to the point where they are unrecognizable. He's infuriating that way. But, on the other side, he's clearly a very successful con man who has managed to make a lot of money and has built up this incredible waste of time and effort in Kentucky to support his beliefs. So that's kind of impressive.

. . .

Let's talk a little bit about your visit to Ham's Creation Museum. How did that come about and what was that like?

How it came to be was, I was going to be in Columbus for a meeting of the SSA and I talked to a few people, and I suggested as long as we're in Ohio and as long as Kentucky's just across the river there how about if we make a trip? And people were agreeable and we signed up a whole bunch of students—atheist students—who were interested in going. So we brought three hundred people to the Creation Museum.

What was it like in there? Oh, in some ways it was extremely disappointing because, basically what it is, is...you've heard of those hell houses they have on Halloween? You know, those haunted houses where it's a guided tour all through all the horrors of modern life? That's what it is. It's not a museum, if I contrast it, for instance, to the American Museum of Natural History, which right now I think is probably the best museum for learning about evolution. The AMNH has this beautiful set of displays where you just kind of wander through and they lead you, not step by step, but through the logic of what they're talking about and they give you examples and they show you evidence. Ken Ham's Creation Museum is nothing like that. It is basically a canned tour. You take a little serpentine trip through their so-called museum and they lead you through all these exhibits. Half the exhibits are not about science at all but to tell you that you're doomed if you believe in evolution and can go to hell. Americans are doomed.

Kids are ruined by this, with all that kind of crap. And when you do look at their so-called science exhibits they are extremely poorly done. They don't explain anything. Here's the situation, this is our answer. For example, one thing that I thought was hilarious, was they explained how all the animals got from the ark after the flood was over and they've got these dioramas and these displays showing floating rafts of debris that the animals would hop on and they'd go wandering off to Australia or New Guinea or South America or whatever. It's full of bogus arguments like that. Just sort of ad hoc explanations for how you can reconcile the book of *Genesis* with the actual facts, even though they ignore most of the actual facts.

Now that Ham has put together his ark, have you considered taking a trip to that?

I am. I'm sort of planning on it. This summer there's a meeting of the Genetics Society that's taking place in Cincinnati and I've got a student who's going to present there, and so we were actually thinking, we'll go there, we'll do the science thing, and then we'll make a little afternoon trip over to Noah's Ark. I'll take some pictures and laugh at it.

I know you've been asked this so many times, but I've got to bring up the Eucharist controversy, which I think is hilarious. What were your motivations to do that?

It was a conscious effort to distract from something going on down in Florida, I think it was, where a student who had innocuously taken away a piece of the communion wafer to show to a friend who was at church with him.

And the congregation just went nuts. They were screaming, yelling, and trying to claw it out of his hands and treating it like some magic thing that needs to be protected and then afterwards all these people were coming along deploring and weeping and crying about how this kid had defiled Jesus and had kidnapped Jesus and was torturing Jesus and it was just ridiculous. I said this doesn't make any sense. You're fine to have your Communion ceremony. I'm not opposed to Catholics having whatever rituals they want as long as they don't harm anybody, but we have to draw the line when a religion tries to dictate to non-believers what they must do in their own homes and their own privacy. And when they try to impose these absurd mythological ideas on individuals and say to people, who don't believe in them, that no, you have to respect our particular magic ceremonies, or you're a bad person. And, that was the entire motivation to say okay, that's ridiculous. I can do anything I want to a cracker. It's not illegal. I don't even consider it disrespectful. It would be disrespectful if I walked into a church and disrupted a ceremony, but having a cracker at home and throwing it in the trash? No, you can't possibly complain about it.

I was wrong, of course. People did complain about it, and they complained about it rather loudly for quite a while. But the point I was trying to make is, no, you don't have a right to interfere in people's lives.

I understand you got some death threats over that.

Oh, I get death threats all the time. They've sort of become the background of my life. There were a number of them at that time. Like I said, nowadays mainly I'm getting them from atheists, but numerous Catholics were very upset with me.

The University of Minnesota at Morris was supportive of you, and I think that's great. Was there ever any concern about how things were going to go down with them?

Sort of. I wouldn't exactly say supportive. What it was is that the University system as a whole has a commitment to free speech. As long as I'm not doing something illegal, I'm not harming people, they're going to support the right of a tenured faculty professor to speak out. It's not like they agreed with me;

what they agreed with was the principle that I have the right to say these things and that's what they supported.

I don't want to give the impression that the University of Minnesota is chomping at the bit, anxious to get out there and desecrate wafers or something, but they are very committed to making sure that the faculty have a voice, and so I applaud them for that. They were very good about that. I had a number of conversations with lawyers here who were supportive in the sense that yes, you can do this, we're not going to tell you to stop but there are boundaries.

They didn't have to say this, but I knew not to go marching down to the Catholic Church and do things. But at home, as long as I'm not pretending to represent the University as well, because the University was not doing this, it was just me personally.

In 2013, you publicly divorced yourself from the skeptic movement and I wondered if you wanted to talk a little bit about that. What led to that decision?

Oh, a number of things. Organized skepticism has been distinct from organized atheism and they both have serious flaws. They both have representatives who are not quite committed to the true principles that they should be committed to. Skepticism has a long history of drawing boundaries. So, the organized skepticism movement, organizations like SciCop and so forth have long claimed that there are certain things that are outside their purview that they will not criticize things that lack evidence, for instance. And so they've always been careful to separate themselves from criticism of religion. Because what they do is well because religious claims don't even have grounds to say that there's evidence to be tested, it's all accepted on faith so it's not something that we can test.

This has always irritated me because in science this is not the way things work. If you have a hypothesis that has no evidence for it, it is not treated as something that...well, we just ignore that then, if you're proposing it. You can pretend that it doesn't exist. Because if you've got people who are advocating for a badly-formed hypothesis that is so bad that you can't even test it, we can rightly say that's an untestable piece of crap and we're not going to accept that. And it's the same way with religion. Religion is, if it's true, faith based, right? It's just people's feelings about stuff. And I would say that yes, if you're in the privacy of your home, if you're in a group of people who share these beliefs, that's fine. I'm not bothered by this. It's just that religion at the same time has been pushing to get this stuff into public schools, to dictate common government policy. It's a whole bunch of biases there that the skeptic movement for a long time was resentful about and didn't want to do anything about it. And it got to the point where they were actually disavowing atheism because they said that wasn't good skepticism which is utter nonsense.

A number of years ago, for instance, there were a number of skeptics, particularly skeptics who associated with the amazing meeting which was going on at that time, who were peevish about the Skepticon conference, because Skepticon didn't have that bias. They had no problem inviting a bunch of atheists to speak there and to speak about atheism. But they declared that's not true skepticism; that's an atheist conference, so you can't call yourself Skepticon, which is just absurd. It's just one of those many things that finally got me fed up and I said nope, I want nothing to do with us.

So do I still consider myself a skeptic? Skepticism as a philosophy is perfectly legitimate, but organized skepticism is a mess with a lot of historical baggage that I find extremely objectionable, and I want nothing to do with it.

What exactly went down with Atheist Ireland?

I have no idea. That was a weird one. Yes, I gave a couple of talks at Atheist Ireland meetings and then what kind of gradually emerged, every time I gave a talk at these meetings, the head of Atheist Ireland, Michael Nugent, would always take me aside and berate me and tell me I was too mean. I was too rude, I kept saying these awful things about people and I needed to stop. I've already admitted I'm abrasive and aggressive and that's just the way I am and that wasn't going to change. So finally he just decided he wanted nothing to do with me and didn't like me and started writing all these things about me. In particular he was taking innuendo and slander from some of those weird people who hate feminism and hate social justice and repackaging it and saying these verbal things are true about PZ Myers. They weren't, but he would make these arguments. He basically got deranged and obsessive about me. So I have nothing to do with him anymore or Atheist Ireland, which is a shame because Ireland is a lovely country. I'd love to go back there, but I'm not going to be participating in anything with Atheist Ireland.

You've won numerous awards and have even had an asteroid named in your honor. What do you feel is your proudest achievement so far?

My proudest achievements are marrying the love of my life and having three kids who grew up to be wonderful people. That's the stuff that matters.

GREYDON SQUARE

Best known as an atheist emcee hailing from Compton, California, Eddie Collins works under the name Greydon Square. An Iraq war veteran and outspoken atheist, he majored in both physics and computer science in Phoenix, Arizona. Influenced by groups as diverse as Phil Collins, Stanley Clarke, and fellow Compton resident DJ Quik, Greydon Square released his first album, *The Compton Effect*, in 2007. After being approached by a handful of labels, he opted to distribute the album through his own company. The following year, he released his second album, *The CPT Theorem*. The music on these two albums mostly dealt with philosophical questions, and Greydon established himself as a talented emcee with a flair for multi-layered lyrics.

He is a member of the international secular hip-hop activist movement The Anti-Injustice Movement, and has also established his own organization, Grand Unified Theory, which "uses creativity to educate people about science and rational thinking."

Greydon Square has since released three more albums,

Type I: The Kardashev Scale, Type II: The Mandelbrot Set, and *Omniverse: Type III*.

* * *

I understand you grew up as a Christian. Is that true?

I grew up as a Christian simply because I was told I was a Christian growing up. I've always maintained that I was taught about religion when I was intellectually defenseless by people who had an intellectual advantage over me. They were telling me these things. Being a child and asking, "Where does the universe come from?" These people told me their answer to that, and they did it with such a definitive amount of certainty, they did me and a lot of other kids in similar situations a great disservice. They taught me under the same circumstances that they had been taught. I always maintain that I was taught to think and believe what every other black kid who was a black kid in America was taught to believe—the monotheistic Judeo-Christian belief system.

At what point did you begin to question religion?

I had already come back from Iraq. I had already been deployed, and had that experience in Iraq, so I was pretty shaken by what had happened over there. It wasn't really until I had been going to school out here in Arizona, when I started studying physics and philosophy—I started reading more secular skeptical authors. The Dan Dennetts, the Christopher Hitchens, even W.B. DuBois.

What made you come up with the idea of combining your love of hip-hop music with atheistic subject matter?

I had always been into hip-hop. I grew up on it. It's a part of my culture. So growing up on hip-hop is one aspect of it. Just knowing that form of communication to communicate my form of ideas, my struggles, and my hurts, was already there. What made me sort of turn my focus to religion and the dissection of religion, I'd say that came when I was about twenty-six. I'm thirty-four now, but there was a time there where I was struggling with what I believed, and not being totally sure what I believed, because I had been told for so long what I believed.

How difficult is it to find a black audience as an atheist hip-hop artist?

How difficult is it? It's *very* difficult, but it's only difficult because black people have been lied to about the merits of education and skepticism and what it means to be critically-minded and what critical thinking is and what proper reasoning skills are. Black people have been done a major disservice because for a long time this religion was used to control them. The idea of questioning without questioning—a kind of obedience without questioning comes from this idea of being a former slave. You never questioned the slave master; you never questioned the overseer, who just happens to be the preacher or whomever. Obviously he's the gateway to god.

Why do you think it's easier for a black audience to digest black Muslim messages in hip-hop—I'm thinking of Ice Cube in the early '90s—than it is to digest atheistic messages?

Let's look at that. First of all, that's a great question. Especially the reference you used, because I grew up on Ice Cube. For me, I looked at Ice Cube not necessarily as a guy who is accepting Islam—the Nation of Islam, which is not really Islam the way that we understand it. It's been changed and bastardized into some other shit that certain blacks use as a method of political gain and that type of stuff. That's a whole other conversation.

I think the answer more directly is that atheism and non-belief is seen as being unnatural, because god is considered the most natural expression of nature for most people who think about gods. Black people, with our knowledge and understanding that the first man was African, we kind of take this idea from there and kind of disassociate ourselves from what our original beliefs were. There are many reasons as to why black people are more open to any type of theistic message as opposed to nature. We feel that as the original man on earth, we were the closest to the expressions of nature. Therefore, for us to be completely absolvent of that natural expression that we believe exists, is somewhat an affront to the senses of the African. The African was a very spiritual person, a lot like the native American, and the Aborigine, and whatever ancient man you can pick out of a hat. But that spiritualism, that relationship to nature where that spiritualism was derived from...

We were a polytheistic people. We had a bunch of different gods. I actually had a conversation with a young black man in Long Beach about a week ago. He said, "Just because we believed in multiple gods didn't make it right." And I had to stop before I went into this whole other part of this conversation about relative right and wrong. You'll question if worshiping multiple gods is right or wrong, but you won't question the god who created the place of eternal damnation and torture? As if that's not something to be questioned.

Do a lot of rappers want to beef with an atheist hip-hop artist?
No, they want to be a champion for their belief system. I

guess it's the same thing in the end. When people try to come at me or take shots at me, they don't ever do it directly. Because number one, I don't think they want a direct confrontation with me lyrically, based on my terms. Hip-hop is very political in that way. People look at people who are adversaries or rivals and they say, "Who started it? Why was it started? Is this person talking shit? Was this person minding his own business? What happened?" So someone can feel justified in saying, "You got your ass kicked because you deserved it. You got destroyed in a rhyme because you deserved it." For me, the only way I'm ever going after someone directly is if they come after me on my terms. No one is going to challenge me on some atheistic "I wanna battle you on religion" sort of thing. Nobody. Because I've literally made a career out of it. I'm good at it. So for me it's like, do they wanna beef? No, I don't think they wanna beef. I just think they want to be looked at in their communities as champions of their belief system, whether that's Islam or Christianity or whatever.

Do you get much hate mail?

Not anymore. I'm sure I'm not even relevant enough anymore for hate mail. It's a different time now. Back in the day in 2006, 2007, I was coming back from Iraq three years prior. I was talking about people who were off limits as far as what you could say about them. People were very afraid of saying things about Islam, saying things about the tenants of Islam that were ridiculous, or Mohammad, or whatever. Remember, "Draw Mohammad Day" was a big thing back then. And now it's like, "You're still doing Draw Mohammad Day?" It's a different time. Now we've switched to where radical Islam is no longer the enemy. Now it's the patriarchal nature of society. Now feminism is the one that's driving the vehicle. So it's not really looked at the same, where if I write a song about Islam today as opposed to the way it was six years ago.

Do you see yourself as an atheist activist?

I see myself as a voice for critical thinking and skepticism. Atheism is a result of my critical thinking and skepticism. But I don't champion atheism today the way I once did. And that's partly a personal issue with me concerning the atheist community. I feel that the people who make up the atheist community are very biased and very closed-minded. They don't like a certain level of urban involvement, whether it be from people like me who come from the inner city, and not some white guy from some place who wrote a book. I'm a black dude from Compton who raps. And I'm hardcore... I don't sound cheesy when I do it.

With no disrespect, if it's a white guy who doesn't come from the hood, it's like, "Sure, come to our atheist conventions. You don't threaten us." But Greydon Square? People know he'll punch you. If something happens, you still get that little hood element. It doesn't matter if I'm an atheist, I'm still from Compton. I still grew up in a time where if you said the wrong thing, I'd punch you in the face for it. And not a lot of people would agree with that. Not a lot of people would be like, "Oh, this is the right thing to do." It's not about being right or wrong. It's the lens through which I see the world. So I understand why certain atheist groups are like, "We don't really wanna deal with Greydon like that."

Not that I'm acting crazy at performances or anything like that, but I do feel like there's a certain level of sorting that goes through the people they want to allow in that community to represent that community. I don't see many dark faces that represent that community. So I don't champion atheism the way I did back in the day, because I thought this was something we could all get behind. "This is something we could all get behind and be down for each other if someone attacks me." But then I found out it was mostly atheists who talk the most shit about me—because I was a rapper. Because I wanted to rap about my skepticism, then it wasn't valid. If I was writing a book, then all of a sudden that makes it more valid.

You joined forces with other atheist emcees on the song "2013 Atheist Dreadnought." How did that track come together, and what was that experience like?

Well, there have actually been several "Atheist Dreadnought" songs. There was the 2008 version, the 2010, 2013, and most recently 2016. I have a method in which I make my music. A lot of times I will make songs that are independent, and a lot of times there are songs that I make that are considered legacy. My legacy songs are based on earlier ideas that have evolved into a new sound or new opinion that I rewrite for the record. I did a song called "Squared" all the way back in the day, and I talked strongly about atheism. Then I did a song called "Cubed" that was an evolution of that. So "2013 Atheist Dreadnought" was simply an evolution of the legacy song. And the legacy idea behind the dreadnought was, you know, a dreadnought was this big battleship in the war, and I was always a big fan of starships and any type of ship where there was a captain and a crew. So I always liked the idea of leading my crew on a ship to tackle the task at hand. Those songs were always meant to be like this is a captain and his crew. They're on an away mission, and they're basically rapping from this perspective of guys who are dismantling religion.

As for how the song came together, I'm the executive producer for all my music, so I have to personally arrange the song, arrange all the people, get all the people to agree, figure out who's available and what kind of equipment they have. I'm also the executive producer and lead engineer on all my music, so I have to get the files and import them, mix them myself, cover up anybody's bad qualities on the recording. It was one of the times where I had told everybody I was doing a continuation of the song. I basically told them, "This song is going down in a couple of months, so I'm going to hit you guys up. I'll send you a beat and let you know." And sure enough, I got the beat and I knew that was gonna be it just from the energy it had. And I knew that song was going to be one of the singles from that album because that album didn't have as much atheism in it as previous albums had. I had made an active approach to not put as much direct atheism into my music as what I had done before. And that was one of the songs where I kind of broke that rule.

To be honest with you, I think "Atheist Dreadnought 2016" is better. That's not to say that one is worse, but I definitely feel like 2016 is much more aggressive and much more brutal in regards to how we go at certain things in society—not just religion.

You recorded the song "War Porn" with Canibus, who is another emcee I respect. What was Canibus' demeanor like in regards to your beliefs, and what was that experience like?

First and foremost, I want to pay my proper respects to Canibus. I consider him, if not the greatest rapper of all time, one of the greatest rappers of all time. He is a grandmaster in skill and craft. And I feel like he got a raw deal when it came to hip-hop and how they treated him. They were all intimidated by his intelligence. I know people who came right out and said it.

Having said that, 'Bis with me was cool. I had no problems working with him. The first time we spoke, we didn't even talk about music. We talked about our experiences in the military. We were both in the Army around the same time. We talked a lot about being soldiers and living in the barracks. That kind of led to conversations about spirituality and religion and aliens and stuff like that. I gotta say, people have this opinion about Canibus that he's crazy and that he believes in weird stuff. You know, he really doesn't believe in anything crazier than anyone else I've heard. He just happens to believe in much less popular things. He talks about things like MKUltra, the C.I.A., the psychedelic program. That's not conspiracy talk, but Canibus gets lumped into this "conspiracy nut" thing. "He's crazy." He's just talking about stuff that most ignorant assholes don't know anything about. Sure he makes some wild accusations about hip-hop and the politics in it, but whatever.

I always look at him as a guy who has an incredibly deep mind. He's maybe the most intelligent rapper I ever heard. He's the reason I started rapping. Any conversation we ever had, I always assumed the role of pupil and conceded the role of teacher to him and his vast intellect.

In the past you've said you believe people are having a "dishonest conversation" when it comes to theism vs. atheism. What did you mean by that?

With theists and atheists, I think there are two different starting points. Atheists start from the perspective of asking the questions and letting the data dictate their overall hypothesis of what they think is, whether it be observational direct or indirect evidence to build some sort of hypothesis. Theistic minds start with a conclusion. They start with this premise, and the assumption is this; that God existed and then created some stuff. We start from two different places, and we don't even acknowledge that when we get into the debate. My job is not to disprove a god to you. The theist's position most of the time is to prove why their beliefs are not ridiculous...why their beliefs are valid. To me, the secular position is simply saying, "That's a nice story you have. I just don't believe it." It's like, "That's a nice story you have about having a million dollars in the bank, but until I see an ATM receipt I'm just going to take it as a story." I don't believe most people's story when they say they have a million dollars in the bank. That's not to say I couldn't be wrong, but until presented with evidence I'm not going to believe it. And they think when you don't believe something, then it's a direct indictment on what they believe. "If you don't believe it, then that must mean you don't respect the fact that I believe it." That's not even true. I don't respect the belief itself, but I respect *your* belief. I just don't respect the belief that people are going to go someplace where they're going to be tortured for all of eternity just because they didn't think a certain way.

AUTUMN CHRISTIAN

Autumn Christian is a talented up-and-coming fiction writer from Texas making a name for herself with such titles as *We Are Wormwood*, *The Crooked God Machine*, and *Ecstatic Inferno, & Girl Like a Bomb*. She says she has been told reality is that which, when you stop believing in it, it doesn't go away, so she is waiting for the day when she hits her head on the cabinet searching for the popcorn bowl and all consensus reality dissolves.

She's been a freelance writer, a game designer, a cheese producer, a haunted house actor, and a video game tester. She considers Philip K. Dick, Ray Bradbury, Katie Jane Garside, the Southern gothic, and dubstep to be her primary sources of inspiration.

* * *

What kind of atmosphere did you grow up in, in terms of religion?

I was born in Oklahoma. I grew up in Fort Worth, Texas, so

it was a protestant Christian background, and pretty much everyone I knew was conservative. I didn't really know any alternate viewpoints from that.

When did you come to the realization that you were an atheist?

It was a gradual thing that happened over the course of my teenage years. I think it really started to happen when I was fourteen. It kind of feels like this process of disillusionment. Also, having a bad break-up, you start to realize there's cracks in the foundation of this logic, and it was something I had assumed was real from a very young age, but I was also into trouble a lot, because I was a very curious person. I was in private school, and I found out soon that people wouldn't ask questions, because it reveals the inadequacies in their logic. Ultimately, I became an atheist because there is no proof in God. If there was proof in God, I would cease to become an atheist, but since there is no proof, there is no practical reason to believe.

Were there any particular things you read or were introduced to that helped sway you closer to the light?

I think it's interesting that you mention that, because I think it was the Bible for me. As I got older, I got more devoted and wanting to learn about Christianity, but I found that the more I read, the more confused I became. Especially reading the Old Testament, and you'll see God is a violent killer, and a God who doesn't ascribe to his own rules. And we're all taught that God is loving and cares about us, but the reality looks much different when viewed inside the Bible.

. . .

You mention growing up in Oklahoma. Where are you now?
　　I actually live in San Diego right now, but I spent most of my adult life in Austin, Texas.

Austin's fairly liberal, right? Better than Oklahoma?
　　Yeah. It's kind of a little blue dot in a sea of red.

You're also bisexual. Was your family more upset by the news that you were bisexual, or that you were an atheist? Or did they care?
　　I felt like they were more upset by the atheism because I had tried to keep that hidden for a long time. And, of course, that's more of a damning thing. You're essentially saying your child is being sent to hell, as opposed to, "well, this is a sin, but we can look past that."

A lot of us flirt with agnosticism at one point before we become a full-fledged atheist. Did you ever have that period?
　　I'm an agnostic atheist. I can't say for sure, but I'm positing that there is no god. I think a lot of people see agnosticism as sort of an in-between point. And there was a point after where I was not believing in Christianity anymore, that I was looking into paganism, and all these other kinds of "new age" spiritual things. But the more I read about different religions, the more I saw their fallacies were all the same.

Religion and why people believe was of interest to you at one point. Is that still an interest to you?
　　Yeah. I think it's really fascinating actually, because when

you think about religion, it was before we had science as a tool. I felt that at one point it was a very useful way to help humans evolve consciously because, as far as you know, you're the only intelligent thing in the universe, and you extrapolate from that, "there must have been something bigger than us" whether or not that's true, and then use that as a narrative of who you are and where you're going. That's a very important part of being human, having that narrative of your life and what the purpose is.

Do you see religion as being a good thing or a bad thing? Can it be a good thing, or is it pretty much always a bad thing?

It's both. It's kind of like Nietzsche said, I think it's in *The Gay Science*, "God is dead" because the Age of Enlightenment had come, and we were casting off old ideas of religion. The problem was that religion, at least from that perspective, gave us morality, and if we had no morality, then who are we, and where are we going? And that can be both a good thing and a bad thing because it means either that we're either going to be our own salvation or we're going to be doomed.

Atheists often handle their atheism in different ways. Are you an outspoken and militant atheist, or do you hide it unless you're asked? How do you generally approach that?

That's changed over the years. When I first became an atheist, I was very outspoken and I was very angry. I noticed a lot of these atheists who used to be Christians are very angry at God, the God that doesn't exist, because they're being let down about all of existence. I would be confrontational, I would argue with people, they would say I didn't respect them, and I would say, "Well, you want me to die and go to hell so how can we be on equal footing?" I actually wrote a book called *The Crooked God Machine*, which was a sci-fi dystopian book about a terra-form planet. It's core was being run by a machine that was shown as a god because there was actual proof there was a thing that was helping humanity progress and not fall into chaos, but then it goes horribly wrong because the God in the Old Testament has a very twisted perspective of how things should be run.

I think as I've gotten older, I'm less confrontational, just because I've seen how it affected status. When someone challenges an idea, we get this theological response that we're being typically threatened. I think a better way is to have the information if somebody would come and be interested in reading or looking at it, and being less directly confrontational.

Aside from The Crooked God Machine, *how else has your atheism affected your writing?*

There's a sci-fi writer named Ursula Le Guin. She's also an atheist sci-fi writer, and she has a quote that says basically the role of the writer is to find the questions that are unanswerable, and answer them. I feel like books teach us how to be human. It's sort of like a more advanced way of play, like when you see dogs playing and they're learning how to engage in the real world and fight without the consequences. With humans, one of the ways we learn is through error, but we can't learn everything through error, and that's where things like books come in and we get the knowledge of how other people lived and it's possible to live through their experiences, and that becomes our experience.

I think I'm most interested in the question of *how* do we live after God. I think morality is a biological imperative because there's something in us that was telling us "these need to be the core tenants to save" and these are the things that humans need to follow. Like, we need to not kill people, we need to not steal, these are good ways to learn how to become a human. We don't necessarily know the mechanisms of what that is that's telling us that in our brain, but I think that's an important thing to explore -- who are we without God, and what is truth for us.

What are your views on the prevalence of Christianity in American society?

I think it's dangerous. I think a lot of people have this "live and let live" attitude about that. Like the 'coexist' bumper sticker. It's funny, because most of those religions are monotheistic and aren't tolerant of all the other religions. It's this weird cognitive dissonance, where we can all live together and be peaceful, except the core tenants of some of each state, and exactly the opposite of that. Some of these religions are telling us how to live in ways that aren't really agreeable to people who have different viewpoints. Like whatever your belief is on abortion and women's rights, the immigration thing, which I've seen being attributed to different religious texts, but as far as I know, there isn't much of a religious basis for that. And just the way that people use cognitive dissonance to protect their religious beliefs is a dangerous way of thinking, and it's not a way of thinking that can be relegated to a small part of your brain. You can't just be like, "I'm going to be rational about everything, except religion" because our brains don't work like that. I think it's dangerous in the sense that we're not always using logic to try to come to consensus on the problems that we have. We're using more of the feeling and the tribalism.

. . .

Now that you live in a more liberal place, and you're an atheist, what does your world look like? Do you live in a bubble? Are you surrounded by people with similar beliefs?

I actually do live in a bubble. I'm a writer, so I spend most of my time by myself, and my partner, he's an atheist, too. We have similar values. I don't run into a lot of Christians on a day-to-day basis, and if I do, we generally don't talk about religion. The internet is sort of self-selecting, and the algorithms have narrowed our views to show us similar things to our interests. I try to friend different kinds of people on Facebook, but I find that those self-select themselves out of my friend pool, or I just won't see those [religious] people.

You mentioned your boyfriend being an atheist. The main thing I've seen as a single atheist, it's usually the other person who says, "I can't date you." Before you met your boyfriend, would you have dated a Christian, or did you rule that out?

I don't want to say for sure, but I feel like the answer would be no, just because the way we thought about life and wanted to structure our family would be fundamentally different. I can't imagine that a Christian would be okay with me going to hell, from their perspective.

Have you had many bad experiences with people once they've found out you're an atheist?

I have had bad experiences with my family, but I don't want to get into specifics, in case they're listening to this. I think it's mostly the people closest to you who are the ones that are going to get the angriest because they feel like your eternal soul is in trouble.

Before I was a writer, I worked in game development, and

generally, I feel like game development is more liberal and more secular, so I never really ran into huge problems with that.

As far as religious people see atheists, they have a lot of misconceptions about us. In your experience, what do you see as the biggest misconception about atheists? Or is there a particular one that annoys you?

One thing that I've seen is that people think we're all like Richard Dawkins. We're all angry, usually white people, usually male, and jerks. And that we're immoral. It's funny, because I was just looking up stats on religion. Atheism—I think Islam surpassed it in the last few years—atheists used to be the most hated group in the country because people think they're going against the values of America, which is funny because the founding fathers were not Christian. I think the biggest misconception is that without God, there's nothing keeping us from being serial killers or burning the world down, but morality is also a biological imperative, so it's difficult to explain that to people.

SHANNON LOW

Shannon Low started playing music at the age of ten in his school band. His love of music eventually led him to begin playing metal music around 2001. He played guitar for two different bands in the early 2000s. In 2008, he and guitarist Bryan Cox formed the Christian band The Order of Elijah, which featured what frontman Low has called "crazy ass screaming metal music." A year later they played their first gig. Low also played guitar for the worship band at Ignite Church in Joplin, Missouri for a number of years. The Order of Elijah released their first album, *Accession*, independently in 2012. The following year they signed with Rottweiler Records, who then released newly re-recorded versions of the songs from the previous album on *Dethrone*, along with a few new tracks. This would be their first national release. In 2015, these self-proclaimed "bad boys of Christian music" left Rottweiler and signed with Luxor Records, releasing the album *War at Heart*.

In May 2016, the Christian rocker made news when he announced on the band's Facebook page that he has lost his religion and now considered himself an atheist.

* * *

Tell me about your history with religion.
My family was never really religious, but they sent me to church. I went to church on a school bus when I was younger. But I didn't get baptized until I was twenty. Just shortly after that was when I started getting really passionate about it. I went through the roller coaster of life—up and down. I always believed, but it took about eight years before I was part of a church. I was kind of a late bloomer.

You've said that you saw Order of Elijah as a ministry. Would you please talk about that.
When we first started the band... I had actually left the band I was in before that because I felt that band wasn't letting me represent god. I just played the guitar. Shortly after leaving that band, I formed this one with my guitarist, Bryan Cox. I wanted this to be a ministry. I'd say that first album was really more of that mindset.

I understand the church you were going to in Joplin, Missouri, was pretty fired up. What was that environment like?
Yeah, they're fired up. They're kind of a controversial church themselves. They made the news because they gave away an AR-15 assault rifle for Father's Day. They made the news for that. They were kind of known for having some edgy sermons that were about sex and stuff like that. I mean, they weren't a real charismatic church—there wasn't anyone who ran around or flopped around in the front of the church or anything like that.

. . .

I've been told that there are sex and drugs in the Christian music scene. Can you confirm or deny that?

Some Christian bands are a little more straight-edged than others. I've met Christian bands who were like us; they would drink and party it up when they were out on tour. We never did a lot of that, but we did drink if we did a bar show or something like that. We've never been really crazy. But there are straight-edged Christian bands out there who pray two or three times before their shows... They won't be drinking or doing any of that stuff. You know, show me a hundred different Christians and I'll show you a hundred different Christianities.

What factors led to your loss of your faith?

For me it began with the Bible. I started investigating bad stories I found in the Bible. I wasn't falling for the apologetics. That was a tipping point. And I started researching a lot about the history of the Bible itself and how it was written. When you start learning about stuff like Constantine and when the books were written, even if a person stays in their faith after that, it's almost impossible to not perk your ears up when you hear that and be like, "What?" Some people will follow the reason where it leads them, and other people just choose to dig their heels in deeper.

A lot of the articles I read credited Richard Dawkins as being a big part of your conversion to atheism. How big a role did Dawkins' work play in that?

Well, it's been good click bait on the Internet to really credit that to Dawkins. It doesn't upset me whenever I see that. I've seen all different types of titles as to how the articles have been portrayed. It's just a catchy line to get people to read the story. In the end, it was, for me, the Bible. It's just impossible to look through it and take it seriously with a reasonable mind. I will say that when I read *The God Delusion* I considered myself an agnostic. I remember the lady whom I bought it from asked me if I was an atheist, and I told her I was agnostic. But after reading *The God Delusion*, I just understood what the titles meant a little bit better. One of the things it explained about agnosticism is that if you boil it down...the person who claims to be an agnostic is getting their ideas of whom this god might be from religion. It's still a link tying you to a hope that it might be real. In the end, you can ask them if they think Christianity is real, they'll say, "No, there's no way that can be real." What an agnostic is really saying is, "Every idea you've given me of god, I don't believe. But there might be a chance. I don't know, maybe there really is a god."

If there was a group of people who worshiped aliens or a people who believed in faeries who perform magic and we can't see, then you'd be agnostic toward faeries. Or you'd be agnostic to aliens creating us. One-third of Ireland believes in leprechauns. I'm sure that two-thirds of Ireland is agnostic to leprechauns. [Laughs.] If someone was raised up to believe in no gods at all, then there wouldn't even be a reason to be an atheist. There's kind of a paradox in the title of agnosticism. Atheism means you have rejected the gods that have been held up before you. At the end of the day, I think agnostics are really atheists.

I have always found it humorous that most Christians believe atheists know nothing of the Bible, when in reality, most atheists know the Bible far better than the Christians themselves.

It's where you've been brought up. People tell me, "I see the proof of god whenever I read the Bible. When I read the scripture, it gives me peace and solace." Well, I have a Muslim friend who finds peace and solace whenever he reads the Quran. I mean, when we really get down to it, I know people who can read *Harry Potter* and it gives them peace and solace.

I think Christianity has been held above a lot of other philosophies. I personally see Jesus as a philosopher, whether he said all the religious things or whether he even existed or not. His story is not like Socrates', but it has philosophical grounds. I think the glorification of this one person has really put a shadow over a lot of other really great philosophers and many other people who said good things that would possibly be more relevant in today's society. I don't know many Christians who can quote much Gandhi or Buddha, but I'm sure they would agree they had some substantially great things to say about caring for someone else or how to let your anger go. I believe the myth around Jesus Christ has been glorified so much that it's cast a shadow over other things that could possibly help us.

What was the rest of the band's reaction to your coming out as an atheist?

The rest of the band was excited to get away from the Christian title, I'm sure. I was the one driving that. Most of them are agnostic or atheist. We have one member who believes in god, but he's not really religious. They're all really supportive. They're just excited to be playing music. Whenever I posted this stuff on Facebook, they didn't even care. They didn't share the post or anything, so... They already knew everything I typed up. I think they were just waiting for me to tell everyone whenever I was ready. I've been between a rock and a hard place, sort of backed into a corner in regards to "what do I do? What is the message of this band? What do I do?"

It will be interesting to be able to go to a show and not have someone come up to me, asking for me to pray for them, or telling me about their struggles with faith. I find this quite liberating. A lot of people think it's something bad. My decision has really been painted as a bad decision in the Christian community. You know, I find it just as exciting whenever I see someone being skeptical and researching their own doubts as it once was for me to see someone getting baptized and giving themselves to Jesus Christ.

What kind of mail have you been receiving since you came out as an atheist?

Oh, man, we've gotten all kinds of mail. Just everything you can imagine. I opened up some scripture posts today. We still get those. Last night I got some hate mail. The encouraging and positive messages have far outnumbered those though since this has gotten some traction. We've had so many people reach out with their own personal stories, or touching base because they're in a situation where they can't be public about their own atheism. They feel they have to walk around pretending to be someone they're not. Maybe their careers are at stake, or their home life is at stake—something like that. I just try to encourage all those people to be smart about it because it's not worth losing your career or your family life. It's a very powerful statement in the atheist community; the more people who come forward, the less we're gonna be living under this crazy stereotype that we're asshole heathens who go around having orgies and eating babies. I mean, statistics have shown that the atheistic community is more moral than the religious communities by a large percentage. I believe even divorce amongst atheistic couples is quite a bit lower than the sixty-five or seventy-percent divorce rate among Christians.

A lot of Christians believe atheists are just atheists because they've had something bad happen in their lives. Have you heard a lot of that, that you must have had something bad happen in your life that's made you this way?

A lot of people blamed it on my divorce. They think if that never happened, I'd still be a believer. A lot of people have said I never was really a Christian in the first place. I think that's the most common excuse I hear. I think a lot of people don't or can't understand how a person could let go of the thought that there could be a god. I tell them, I saw Sam Harris say once that people tell him they can't imagine what it would be like for nothing to happen whenever you die. And he said, "Well, that's exactly what you said—you probably never imagined it." And if you think about it, it's actually a pretty good probability. That doesn't mean we know what's going to happen, but you can't take it off the table. It's just wishful thinking to say that I know that whenever I die, something will happen. All of these neurons that are firing inside my slushy brain are gonna be downloaded into this ectoplasm soul. You've got to convince yourself of a lot of things to believe that. It's indoctrination from an early age. Even if you're not indoctrinated at an early age, you've grown up around people who are. It's just something that's accepted.

How will this change in mindset inform your new music? Do you see your new music reflecting your atheism, or will you simply make secular music in general?

I've always had somewhat of an infatuation with religion, even when I was a kid and my grandmother was showing me mythology and telling me about Poseidon and Zeus… I've always found that really interesting. I was so passionate about it in the band, and now, even though I feel that I've reprogrammed my mind to have a different view and understanding of how everything works, I will still write whatever's in my heart. On the last album I had a song that was about my daughter. I had a song I wrote right after I shed religion and it was me reflecting on that. The songs' directions could be chaotic—they could go in any direction.

I was thinking about writing a song directly talking to the Christians. A lot of them have been there to support us, but there have been a lot of them who shit all over us from the beginning. Those people put a bad taste for Christianity in my mouth as a whole. I think one of the things that bothers me the most is that the people who do support us say, "Why are you upset with Christianity? Not all Christians are like that." Well, one of my biggest problems with Christianity is that Christians will not stand up to one of their own. Whenever they see another Christian doing something wrong, they just turn a cheek to their own really quickly. As soon as you're doing something they don't like, they let you know, but if they see someone getting out of line who's a part of their culture and a part of their community, they turn away.

Atheists are not that way. Atheists are out there correcting each other all day. I see atheists get into debates themselves. Christians do it too, but usually it's over theological stupid shit; whose apologetic over why this person murdered a bunch of infants in the Old Testament is better. But straight up seeing your fellow Christians saying some really horrible, really mean shit, most of them just sit by idly and keep their mouths shut. Then they want to know why people are getting upset. So there may be a song about that. I'm thinking about calling it "To the Following Christians."

I want people to know that I don't judge who you are by

your beliefs—I judge your beliefs. And people can do that to me all day. In fact, that's all I deal with right now—people challenging my beliefs. Christianity seems to have this awkward immunity—this force field that they've built around them and their beliefs—that says, "You cannot criticize this or this or it's prejudice and rude. It is wrong." Even though the very core commandment unto the disciples was the great commission to spread the word. Make converts. Convince people to believe this religion. That's their main objective. And then they have the audacity to go around and say, "How dare you criticize someone's beliefs?" How can they say that when their belief system is founded on that very principle?

Do you now see yourself as an atheist spokesman?

I think as an artist I'm already considered a spokesman for whatever I choose to talk about. If I'm going to talk about shooting deer, because I like to hunt, which I don't really, then in a way I would be a public spokesman for that. I have a song about my daughter. I suppose I am a spokesman on fatherhood rights, even though I have a really cool ex who doesn't give me any problems about seeing my daughter. So I guess I'm an advocate about many things, and I would say yes, that atheism is one of them.

DAN SAVAGE

Dan Savage is a Renaissance Man of sorts. He's a well-known figure, but is known for different things to different kinds of people. He's a bestselling author, a media pundit, journalist, and LGBT activist. He writes "Savage Love," an internationally syndicated relationship and sex advice column that he initially wanted to call "Hey, Faggot!" in an attempt to reclaim the word for the gay community. He's the editorial director of the Seattle newspaper *The Stranger*, a frequent "Real Time Reporter" on Bill Maher's HBO show *Real Time with Bill Maher*, and the host of a wildly popular weekly podcast, also titled *Savage Love*. He makes frequent appearances on various CNN and CNBC programs, discussing hot button-topics like same-sex marriage and the "Don't Ask Don't Tell" policy. He hosted the MTV series *Savage U*, where he traveled around the country talking to college students about sex, as well as a three-hour call-in show on Seattle radio station KCMU. In addition to these accomplishments, Savage has done things as varied as writing and producing the short-lived ABC-TV sitcom *The Real O'Neals* and working as a theater director.

In 2010, Savage and his husband, Terry Miller, began the It Gets Better Project to combat suicide among bullied LGBT teens. In his writing and appearances, Savage has frequently clashed with both conservatives and the LGBT establishment. He gained his fair share of notoriety when he publicly opposed GOP Presidential candidate Rick Santorum's rather closed-minded views on homosexuality. This eventually led to Savage setting up a website on which he defined the term "santorum" as "the frothy mixture of lube and fecal matter that is sometimes a byproduct of anal sex." In another of his more controversial actions, Savage declared openly that, "I wish the Republicans were all fucking dead." In yet another controversy, Savage once stated that Green Party Senate candidate Carl Romanelli "should be dragged behind a pickup truck until there's nothing left but the rope."

Savage's outspoken rhetoric has not only drawn ire from the Republican Party, but it has also sparked outrage among many Christians. In 2012, Savage, an avowed atheist, ruffled more than a few feathers when he advised a room full of college students they should "learn to ignore the bullshit in the Bible about gay people," prompting many in attendance to leave. He later called the walk out a "pansy-ass move." In 2015, Savage remarked to CNBC talk show host Chris Hayes that the Pope's meeting with noted homophobe Kim Davis emphasized that homophobia "unites people across different Christian faiths." Savage was then predictably criticized for persecuting Christians and bullying the Pope.

* * *

You grew up in the Catholic church. Since then you've stated that you don't believe in any gods. What made you come to this conclusion? Could you talk a little bit about that?

I was one of those kids who had concerns from the very beginning. [Laughs.] In Catholic school they would explain to us that only Catholics went to heaven. Even as a young child, to learn that Gandhi wasn't in heaven, but Hitler could be there if he'd made a confession on his deathbed... That offended my sense of justice and morality, even at that young age. But really it was my sexuality that brought me the conflict or opened my eyes. What happened was, I realized that what the church was telling me, and what my parents were telling me based on what the church told them... what they were telling me about myself was wrong. I just knew it in my bones, so I began to question what else the church might be wrong about. If they were wrong about this, perhaps they were also wrong about virgin births, and people floating up into heaven, and transubstantiation in the Catholic church, and all sorts of other things.

It wasn't long before I started to pull at that thread and the entire garment unraveled. Unlike some people, I didn't make the leap to "what the church tells me about myself is wrong, so I'm going to go to another church that doesn't say that about me." I began to think, why does my church tell me these things? Why did the people who ran the church claim to know these things that they can't possibly know with any certainty? And that's where faith comes in. It just instilled in me this incredible cynicism and doubt about anyone who claims to know anything they can't possibly know. I think there should be humility in the face of the unknowable, and not guesswork that becomes dogma.

. . .

In the past you've talked about Christians bullying gay kids, and Christians have responded by calling you a bully against Christians. What are your thoughts on this?

I read on the Internet that I bullied the Pope! [Laughs.] It's right-wing Christians who say that. It's people who would be unrecognizable as Christians to Jesus Christ. That's right out of the ring-wing playbook; you accuse the other side of that which you know yourself to be guilty of. That's why Donald Trump accused Hillary Clinton of being crooked. That's why Donald Trump was out there talking about a rigged election—because he was rigging the election with the help of the Russians.

So when I say to Christians, "You must not bully gay kids," they turn around and say I'm the real bully. "Quit saying mean things to us!" [Laughs again.] "You're calling us names. You're being intolerant about our intolerance." I put no stock in this argument that right-wing pseudo-Christians make about me being the bully, which is what they say about the whole gay rights movement. They say it's the persecution of Christians. They've had the free hand to persecute queer people for so long that no longer being able to persecute them now makes them feel like they themselves are being persecuted. They say, "We had so much fun burning your houses down for so long, and now we can't do it anymore. How unfair to us! That was an important part of our culture for centuries, and we don't get to do that anymore." So they're sad.

When Christian lawmakers ignore the other so-called abominations found in Leviticus but then point out homosexuality, do you feel they're doing this on purpose? Or do you think they don't actually see the hypocrisy in what they're doing?

Their reading of that is very selective. And hypocritical.

Because when anybody starts to point out anything in Leviticus that they ignore, or anything in the first five books of Moses, they turn around and say, "Well, here's the new testament and Jesus revised all that stuff about women having to live in huts or killing your daughters or virgins on their wedding nights." Somehow that no longer applies. But homosexuality being an abomination still does. They cite that, but when we cite other passages to show how ridiculous this is, then suddenly they don't want anything to do with the Old Testament. Suddenly that becomes the Jewish book, and it's not about Christianity. It happens a lot. They want to have their Leviticus and eat it, too! [Laughs.] They want the bits of Leviticus that apply to others and not to them. This is what the cheap grace of conservative mono-Christianity is all about. If you hate queer people, which means if you aren't queer yourself means no sacrifice, then you're good with God. We saw that with Bristol Palin, leaping from dick to dick from one unplanned pregnancy to the next. But she can still call herself a good Christian because at least she hates gay people. At least she opposes gay marriage. It's this low bar that's very easy to clear, and then you can feel as if you've done everything you can possibly do as a Christian to be right with God. It's so hypocritical.

We have this whole Christian-financed movement to block marriage equality because "marriage is sacred" because of Jesus, because of the Bible. Yet there is no movement to recriminalize divorce, because that might inconvenience straight people, so they're not going to do that.

In 2015, you responded to Ben Carson's assertion that homosexuality is a choice by challenging him to prove it by making the choice and sucking your dick. You caught a lot of flak over that.

Do you regret your choice of words, or are you still pretty happy with that?

Oh God, absolutely not. I actually put it in my book! [Laughs.] Ben Carson wasn't the first. I also issued that challenge to Herman Cain four years earlier when he was running for President. And I issued that challenge to Tony Perkins and some others.

They're constantly invoking gay sex in an attempt to demagogue or stigmatize, and I think it's a good strategy for us to invoke gay sex right back at them. They use gay sex to make the little old ladies who send them checks uncomfortable. So I think we have an absolute right to use gay sex to make them uncomfortable. And it gets to the heart of the matter. That's why that comment took off the way it did both times. I also challenged Mike Huckabee to suck my dick... God, my dick could have been in so many unpleasant places! [Chuckles.]

The reason the comment took off is because isn't because it's profane but because it's called for, because they're the ones saying that gayness is a choice that people make. It's a switch that someone can flip. And they argue that there should be no marital rights for queer people and no gay rights laws because gay people don't have to exist. They say it's just simple and easy because these people could just choose to be straight. Well, if it's simple and easy to choose to be straight, then it must be simple and easy to choose to be gay. So you go ahead and choose it. You show how that's done since sexual orientation is the simple matter of flipping a switch.

To make their argument ridiculous by being graphic and sexual in a conversation that's already primarily about people's sex lives is, I think, completely legitimate. That's why the comment took off and the right wing flipped out, because they knew I had them. It was a solid punch, and it was a punch that landed. That's why they blew it up into this controversy about what a potty-mouthed monster I am. But it didn't work.

Politicians like Mike Pence are in favor of conversion therapy for gay kids. Their religious views won't allow them to believe that being gay can be a natural thing. They see it as a curable sickness. My question is this: what the fuck is wrong with these people?

[Laughs.] I think we see on the right that there's a lot of externalization of internal conflict. Sometimes it's because these people are gay and closeted. When people run around saying sexual orientation is a choice, it's because they've made a choice about sexuality themselves. That's what they're talking about. They're gay and they've chosen not to be out. Like the Marcus Bachmanns of the world, you see people who read as gay, who appear to be gay, and are very vocally anti-gay. They're just scolding themselves. They've externalized that internal conflict.

With others though, you do see this desire to cast around for a scapegoat. Straight people have made a real hash of their own marriages and their own families, and rather than take responsibility for it—instead of asking themselves what they're doing wrong with the heterosexuality stuff—they want to blame gay people. They want to blame this "other." They believe that gay people demanding to be who they are and to live openly and marry and commit and have our own families somehow undermines them and their families. It's ridiculous. Rather than take responsibility, rather than saying to straight people "We've got to get our shit together," they say things wouldn't be so sucky if it wasn't for those cocksuckers over there.

. . .

This current administration promotes religion in virtually every aspect of its function, from a desire to teach it in public schools to their reasoning for various legislative decisions. What do you see as being some of the most dangerous aspects of such actions?

They're divisive. We don't live in a Christian nation. Our founding fathers explicitly stated that fact. Favoring one religion over another is going to create chaos and divide Americans against one another. You look at why faith is stronger in America, why Americans are more religious than Europeans, and one of the answers has got to be that we didn't have a state religion. Religion wasn't about state control. It was about all of us as individuals getting to make up our minds about who our imaginary friends are going to be. Places with state religions, where religion and power are married and joined together—this undermines religion in the long run. So another reason we shouldn't be doing this besides its just being divisive and unconstitutional is, if you're religious, then you should see that it's bad for religion.

So maybe secularists, atheists, and agnostics should cheer these moves where the government promotes one particular kind of religion, because it ultimately undermines religion.

You and your husband adopted a son. Now Republican legislators want to roll back adoption rights for gay couples. What are your thoughts on that?

They're not hurting gay couples. They're hurting kids. Look at Texas. There are more kids in Texas that need homes than there are homes for those kids. Turning away qualified, screened potential parents for these kids because of their sexual orientation or gender identity is just hurting children. You know, a gay couple that lives in Texas and wants to adopt a child can go and adopt in Oregon and then come back to Texas.

Or they can do surrogacy. Or they can have a lesbian friend or a straight friend and create a new kind of family structure that involves more than just a couple. People will find a way to create their families.

What these laws do is they trap children in the foster care system, potentially for the rest of their lives. Everybody who works in adoption will tell you that same sex couples—queer parents—are often willing to adopt the difficult, hard-to-place children that no one else is willing to adopt; older kids, mixed race kids, HIV positive kids, kids who have had alcohol and drug exposure, abused and traumatized kids. A lot of queer parents are willing to take those kids and are happy to adopt them, not because we're satisfied with crumbs, but because often queer parents identify with those marginalized kids. They empathize because they themselves might have been abused for who they are. They might have been discarded by their biological families. So there's an empathy and understanding. To take those parents out of the adoption pool—the couples who are more likely than straight couples to adopt these hard-to-place kids who may never find homes otherwise—is just monstrously cruel. And it's not just cruel to queer couples who can't move or adopt elsewhere, but to the kids who are trapped in Texas' foster care system.

I have a friend who's an evangelical Christian and kind of a fundamentalist. She's a wonderful person and we have the kind of relationship that everybody talks about but few people seem to really be able to have, right? We actually talk over these divisions. We're actually really good friends. I was there for her when the shit hit the fan in her marriage, and she's been there for me when I was really depressed. And she came around on this issue. She knew me after we'd adopted, and that was something she really felt she couldn't get past. I had to explain to her that our son had three chances at a straight couple for parents.

His biological parents couldn't raise him and absolutely did the right thing by putting him up for adoption. And then there were two different straight couples who wouldn't adopt him that he'd been offered to first. They wouldn't adopt him because of alcohol exposure during the pregnancy. And we're the bad guys? We stole him from straight couples who could have raised him? No.

ARON RA

Aron Ra is the president of the Atheist Alliance of America. Previously he was the Texas state director of the American Atheists. In addition, he is the host of the Ra-Men Podcast and the author of *Foundational Falsehoods of Creationism*. A public speaker, video producer, and blogger, Ra is an outspoken critic of Creationism and the director of the Phylogeny Explorer Project.

His blog Reason Advocates, which he co-writes with his wife, Lilandra, formerly appeared at Freethought Blogs and can now be found on the blogging network Patheos. Together with fellow atheist activists Matt Dillahunty and Seth Andrews, Ra was part of the Unholy Trinity Tour in 2014. Ra has held public speaking engagements around the world to discuss atheism and the falsehoods of Creationism.

* * *

I understand you were baptized as a Mormon. Tell me about your history with religion.

I never identified as Mormon, although I was baptized and put in the books as being a Mormon and all that... The reason I never identified as Mormon myself was the same reason that no other person should ever identify as their parents' religion. I think it's strange that I was the only kid who thought like this. How could I know whether or not I'm Mormon if I don't know everything that is required for a Mormon to believe and how would I know that I side more with Mormons than with any other religion since I'd never heard the beliefs of any other religion? So how could I know if I'm Mormon or not? It was just a logical thing to me. Why doesn't everybody ask themselves this question?

Has your family been supportive of your atheism?
I would not say so. [Laughs.] With limited exceptions, they have not been supportive.

What's it like being an atheist activist living in the great big ol' red state of Texas?
It's a very polarizing environment. I'm sure you have the same impression of Kansas... Kansas actually got me started. The Creationist movement in Kansas bled over into Texas with respect to the board of education. Our board of education is actually following yours there in Kansas in what they were trying to do in terms of putting religion into the classroom and politicizing the classrooms. With right-wing Republican religious right dominionists in control of everything at every level, it creates a lot of polarization. When I talk to people from the Northeast, when I talk to people in California, they don't understand why fighting religion is such a big deal. When I talk to people in the South, they get it. My feeling is, much to my

dismay, that the people in the Northeastern states are going to know right where I'm coming from in the next year or so. Because they're finally going to be under that dominionist rule.

You advocated for the inclusion of evolution in the Texas science textbook hearing. Would you talk a little bit about that?

I see Creationism as not just religious, but also not based on science in any respect at all. Science works as the antithesis of faith. They move in exactly opposite directions with completely opposite goals. Everything that would be wrong with science is what religion does. There is the logical fallacy of false equivalents and projection—where they try to project their own faults onto their opponents. They want to paint science as if it were a faith: that you're not believing based on evidence, but believing on faith. Of course that is not the case. They want to say that we're just choosing to believe what we want to believe just as they choose to believe what they want to believe. What I get from religious people is an admission that they believe what they want simply because they have to because they have an emotional attachment...because they were raised to believe that way and they don't want to question it. "Why can't I believe what I want to believe?"

With science, we have a completely different desire. We don't have the desire to believe—we certainly don't have a *need* to believe. Instead we have a desire to understand and to improve understanding. And you can't do that with religious faith because there's no way to show where the errors are or which direction would be correct. You only get that with science. So with evolution, it's certainly not a belief system. There are things that we can prove to be true. And I'm very careful when I say these things. When I say proof I'm not talking about mathematical proof. Absolute proof is something that in positive terms is reserved only for mathematics. I'm using the legal definition of proof where proof would be considered an overwhelming preponderance of evidence. Evidence then also would be a body of facts that are objectively verifiable. Facts are something you can confirm in some way, so you have a body of evidence that are objectively verifiable facts which are positively indicative of, or exclusively concordant with only one available option. You can't have the same evidence for two different mutually exclusive conclusions. Because if the same fact aligns just as well with both options then it's just a fact. It doesn't become evidence until it indicates one or the other. If it's inconsistent with one or indicates the other, then it's evidence.

What religious people want to bring up as evidence for their belief are basically a list of falsehoods and fallacies. Basically they want to bring up every single fallacy they can bring up, including personal incredulity and anecdotal situations like, "Well, I used to be a crack dealer or I used to be addicted to heroin, and then I traded one emotional addiction for another. Now I believe in Jesus and I haven't been stoned since Thursday." That's the kind of thing they present as evidence. That of course does not qualify at all because it's not an objectively verifiable fact and does not positively indicate or is not even concordant with.... Now I can provide all the evidence we need for evolution—all that would ever be necessary. All the facts that positively indicate that and that are only consistent with that. And then I can sit and listen to the crickets when I ask for their evidence. "I used to be a crack whore" isn't going to count. But if that's all they've got. We're done.

What kind of advice would you give to those who would debate Creationists?

Don't. [Laughs.] The problem that most people have when they debate Creationists is that they make the naïve mistake of believing that the person they're debating has some interest in credibility. They don't. They're credulous. They don't care what the truth is.

You can have an honest Creationist. There are people out there who believe in creation, who are honest people and believe for honest reasons—because they've been lied to and they don't realize they've been lied to. It is possible to show somebody the truth and have them realize that they've been misled up to this point. They have to come to a choice very quickly when they end up arguing evolution with somebody who actually knows what they're talking about, like me, who has some background in both evolutionary science and also in theology. Then they've got a problem. Very quickly they're going to have to face the choice to remain honest or whether to remain Creationist. It is no longer possible to be both. They have to concede that macro-evolution has been observed, that there are beneficent mutations, that there are transitional species, and so forth. Or they can lie about that in defense of faith. All too often I've seen people do exactly that.

Professional Creationists—the people who actually make money doing this—all have to lie in order to maintain their positions. They know exactly what lie to tell at what point. So I've made a challenge to people very often when they say that evolution is a hoax.

I say, here's the challenge and it's in two parts. Name one evolutionary biologist or geologist—anyone who's working in a field directly related to evolution—who lied while promoting evolution over creation. Now I'm not saying that there are no scientists who are dishonest. There certainly are, and I can name some off the top of my head. But no, I mean people who have lied in defense of evolution, promoting it over Creationism. And people want to bring up things that just don't work. Like Nebraska Man. I'm sorry, but Nebraska Man is not the name of a scientist. And neither is Piltdown Man. There was one case of an actual fraud, and it was perpetrated *against* scientists, not *by* them. The best that you can say is that the prime suspect was probably not a Creationist. The prime suspect was trying to dupe a museum in hopes of getting some money or notoriety. It was evolutionary scientists who found out the fraud and exposed it. It was not Creationists. Creationists don't know how to expose a fraud—that's why they're still creationists! Creationism is entirely fraudulent.

So name an evolutionary scientist who lied in promoting evolution over Creationism, and tell me the lie verbatim, and explain how we know that it's a lie. It's a very simple challenge. And it's a little bit different from the alternate challenge, which is to name one professional Creationist—anyone who actually makes their money promoting Creationism—ever in history who did *not* lie when promoting Creationism over evolution. You don't even have to go into specifics; just give me the name. Then I'll go through the rest of it to show you the lie and show you how we knew that that guy knew it wasn't true when he said it. And so far, in making that challenge many times, no one has been able to come up with an answer to either question.

They might accuse Ernst Haeckel. But no, that turned out to be a Creationist misrepresenting images that he had worked on in the first edition of his book. They're talking about the drawings that he made that when they duplicate these pictures, and they duplicate them incorrectly, they don't look the same. No, this was a Creationist sham a hundred years after the fact. This was not Ernst Haeckel, and even if Haeckel had faked the drawings it still wouldn't satisfy the question, because it's not promoting evolution over Creationism. There's never been a case where an evolutionary scientist had to do what every professional Creationist always has to do. There's that much disparity.

Creationism doesn't just have any truth; it is based entirely on logical fallacies and fraudulent falsehoods, and that's it.

What are some of the apologetic arguments that drive you the craziest?

[Laughs.] You can go through any list of logical fallacies and you realize that all of them have been used in arguments for god. That's one of the problems. When you argue with someone over Creationism, they don't understand the simplest rules; that anecdotes are not evidence, for example. You know, the things that you cannot reproduce. Such as "my cousin says she saw a ghost." This is not evidence! Changed lives, again, is another one that doesn't count. But why don't they understand that it doesn't count? Or how about "there are so many prophecies."

Well, there's another challenge: show me *one*. And they can't! For instance, they bring up in *Matthew* where it says the birth of Jesus was the fulfillment of this prophecy by Isaiah. No, it's not. Let's go back and read *Isaiah*, and we'll see that he was talking about somebody who was supposed to have been born seven hundred years earlier and was not supposed to be a remarkable person. The only thing about that prophecy was that the king—by the time the child was old enough to choose honey over curds— the king would know that the other kings oppressed against him were no longer a threat. That was the prophecy. Well, that prophecy failed every way a prophecy could fail, because that king ended up killed by the other kings. That prophecy failed nine ways to Sunday. And whoever put it in *Matthew,* saying that this was a fulfillment of the prophecy in Isaiah had obviously not read anything more out of *Isaiah* than one interpretation of one sentence! That clearly doesn't make any sense when you read the rest of the paragraph. The whole Bible is this way. You have to read between the lines and then ignore the lines; just make up whatever you want it to say. This is quite literally what people do.

You've said that Christians don't want to understand the Bible; that they choose to not understand it.

It's make believe. It's not about understanding. It's about pretend. When they say the word "belief," they're using it differently than I would. When I say I believe something, I am saying this is what I believe is most likely the case. But if I believe that, then it means that I can't prove it. If I *can* prove it, it then becomes something that I know. But a believer says he knows things that no one can even know. They certainly don't know, and you can prove it: so it's pretending to know what they don't know. That's what faith is. And then it goes more into it, where they just need to convince themselves this is true. It gets to the point where they either think that if they believe hard enough it will either change reality through the power of positive thought; or if reality doesn't change, it doesn't matter because you've convinced yourself anyway. And this way maybe you won't be afraid of dying because you'll have convinced yourself that it's not really the end.

And I don't understand what the fear of dying is. In Christianity for example, and there are a number of other religions that do this, they tell you that you won't really die. But being dead, being not conscious—it's the same thing when you go in for a surgery. They give you the injection and suddenly you're gone; you don't even have a dream. You're just out. There is no you at all. This is what death is. Death is not something to be afraid of. It really isn't. The fact that you are no longer contributing in other people's lives ...that's a point for some remorse, I guess. But *being* dead isn't the problem. It's *getting* dead. And no religion saves you from that. Regardless of what Christianity wants to promise you, Christians and atheists and Hindus and everybody else runs that risk of lying on the floor, clutching at their chest, and gasping for that last breath.

I'm waiting on a heart transplant, and you'd better believe I've heard about every Christian argument there is to try and make me feel better about my situation. Everybody just assumes that because I'm sick I must be Christian—that I must have help from a higher power.

[Laughs.] I find it so difficult to believe that other people believe this when they tell me what they believe. I'm like, you can't really believe that. And then they hold the same position as me. "I can't believe you don't believe." What? How could I? And this is the question that throws them off. You don't give them the reasons why you don't believe. You put the burden of proof on them because they can never match the burden of proof on *anything*. So if you say, "How could I?," then they have to think of how you could convince yourself that all of this nonsense is true. They know. Not all of them, but there are some who know that they're believing just because they want to. I had one person actually say to me, "You really don't believe?" I said, "Of course not. How could I?" And she said, "I believe because I *have* to." What the hell does that mean? You don't have to. Someone else told me that they know there is a god because they want to see their dead son again after they die. Sorry, but you don't know there's a god. By definition that is not knowledge. That's another logical fallacy, and that's all that there is in support of a god.

. . .

In the past you've said that you believe real explanations are much more rewarding than supernatural explanations. What did you mean by that?

Only accurate information has practical application. There's only so much you can do with a placebo, which is kind of what religion is. It's a soft lie that's meant to make you feel better. Although for most people it's used to manipulate and terrorize them. I see all manner of deception as being a form of violence. Lying is the same thing as violence in the sense that it's something that you might do for self-defense in a desperate situation, but it's something you would want to avoid in all other cases. Because it's considered an affront to someone else. Lying to other people's children in a classroom where they see you as an instructor and they're coming to you for education—is even worse. This is not just child abuse. You're also abusing the child's parents because parents want—or they *should* want—that their children will understand the world that they're going to take the helm of. Children have to have some sort of mastery of their situation before they need to take charge of it. So when you misinform and mislead and misdirect, then these kids have no idea. Then they end up literally wishing upon a star rather than going to see a doctor or having a real solution to any situation.

What do you hope to achieve through your activism?

I need to be completely blunt here. I don't have a lot of hope in achieving anything because my concerns environmentally are extreme. I think we've come to a threshold and we elected Donald Trump at a moment when we didn't have that option anymore. We didn't have another four years to go backwards. So I can't say that I'm very hopeful, because I am aware of how we're overfishing, and... I can't even get into the list of things that I understand that would just sound pessimistic and terrifying. And nobody's taking any of it seriously. But assuming that maybe I miscalculated practically everything—if there's any hope at all—then what I would like to do is to get people to start taking the environment seriously; to start taking education seriously.

I am an anti-theist because I find that religion is a net negative against humanity. Not only does it not have a positive result or reason to be, aside from one or two trivial things—this is at best lipstick on a pig. On the whole, religion is just bad. It's not the source of all evil, but it certainly covers for it. It covers for mental illness and it covers for racism and it covers for every other thing that is wrong with humanity. It makes excuses for it and it enables it. We need to be more humanist, we certainly need to be more rational. I would like to be part of a grassroots change to have a culture that respects literal truth. You know, that you can't just say things are true because you want them to be. It's not truth until you can show that it's true.

That's another one of the rules that I have that people can't seem to follow; I can't say that something is true until I can show that it is true. Otherwise I have to say that it *might* be true. Then with religion the game is to just convince yourself and pretend that it's true even when you know it isn't. It can't be.

You recently announced your intentions to run for the Senate. What are your motivations for throwing your hat into the political ring?

Once again I'm thinking that everything in this state, at every level of government, is run almost entirely by right-wing Republican demagogues and dominionists. Nobody knows what a dominionist is, but it's someone who believes that these are the end days and that what's supposed to happen is that the Christians take over everything and take command of the planet before Jesus comes back. Why? I don't know. But that's the game—take over everything. Abuse the environment as much as possible; reproduce as much as possible; consume all the resources... And you don't have to do anything to help anybody because you can wish upon a star that they'll get the help that they need. And you don't have to atone for anything you've done wrong because you can just say that you're right with your imaginary friend and that he's forgiven you. Then you don't even have to serve jail time for whatever you've done. It's a completely amoral belief system. It's wholly irresponsible and we need to take responsibility. This is what I believe Christianity was designed not to do.

I want to run for office because in two years, when this election happens, I think that after having the majority of the United States in a virtual theocracy, I believe people will start to wake up and start looking to different directions. I don't know what people are going to be thinking about people of my political perspective. I don't know what they think now. I think they think that everybody that is not a believer is somehow a socialist or that socialism is communism—they have all kinds of terrible conceptions about whatever is not the religious right.

I don't know why people want to vote for less government—or think they're voting for less government, but they're always voting for authoritarian candidates who are always as much government as possible in every aspect. They want to govern your bedroom as much as they can. They want to govern in a way that they don't pay taxes and you do. I don't think people understand what less government means. Then they look at me and think that I worship the state or that I must be some kind of a socialist because I think government has a job to do and a responsibility to its people. I want less government than the people who say they want less government! I want the government to get its hands off of people's personal lives.

However, I've also committed the sin of saying that I think rich people should pay their share of taxes just like the poor people. And of course the rich people are in power, so they don't want anything like that.

We have people who say that somehow industry is going to be moral now if you allow the free market. It's going to have some morality that has never existed before. When have corporations ever done the moral or right thing, ever in history? It's not going to happen. It's never happened and it never will. There needs to be regulation on some of this. The founding fathers wrote that the greatest threat against our government was corporations and that they should not be allowed to have power. I didn't even know corporations existed in 1776, but they were aware of that, and they said that the worst thing that could happen to the country was to have corporations come into power. So we are in a very dire situation.

I'm not a pessimistic person. I generally see the bright side of everything. I'm pretty much happy all the time, but as I said, this situation is actually very serious. I shudder that no one else sees that, and in even trying to explain it would make me sound paranoid. So I don't even bother. The best thing that I can do is to be a part of the grassroots resistance and hope that it hasn't gotten to the point where it's too late.

What kind of feedback do you get?
Well, I can say that I frequently get e-mails thanking me for what I'm doing—for changing their minds. There are a lot of times I get people saying they were headed for the priesthood or they believed in the church they were raised in all their lives,

and then they came to this irritating realization because of something I said. It's very nice to hear that.

Surprisingly, I don't get much hate mail from believers. They kind of leave me alone. I actually get more hate mail from other atheists over political differences. There are so many people who can't understand that nobody's going to agree with everybody about everything, and that's okay. You don't have to. If I say the government has, for example, a responsibility to its citizens or a reason to exist at all, then the anarchists will be all over me because in their eyes I worship the state. Everybody wants dichotomous thinking. They can't look at nuance.

I see everyone as being in a u-shaped curve where the vast majority of the population are somewhere out in the middle and it's virtually impossible to be on either extreme. The people I find who are my worst critics are the people who can only see the extremes; you're either all the way on this side or you're all the way on that side... That's never the case! But this is the way that way too many people think now, and I find it disturbing that people think this way.

There's kind of a division in the entire country, and not just in this country anymore I'm sorry to say. There was a time when I was a kid that it seemed like everyone understood that science is real and you'd be crazy to deny what we can show to be real. You'd be crazy to deny science. But at the same time, everybody had this idea that when they died they'd go somewhere. Everybody had both of these beliefs at the same time. It's not like that now. It's an even division pretty much right down the middle of our country. We have religion that's in steep decline in every state and atheism on the rise in every state—at least a third of this country does not believe in a god or anything like that. But at the same time religion is in decline, Creationism is on the rise. How could both of these statistics be true at the same time? It's because you have people who are walking away from religion altogether, and you have people who are walking away from science altogether. There are people walking away from all aspects of science; they're denying climate change, and a hell of a lot of people are arguing that the earth is flat. People are denying their children medical treatment, trying to pray the gay away... You have people turning completely to supernaturalism, and that's half the country. We have a very polarized population.

I would like to think that there's a duality here, that all of them are bad and all of us are good, but I know better. There are a lot of decent people in the religious ranks that have just simply been lied to, and once they realize they've been lied to, then it might have some impact. You have a lot of people on my side of that particular opinion who are no damned good at expressing the common good for the common man. I don't make those same kind of black-or-white judgments that my critics tend to do. I don't put people in the good or bad box, because I know it doesn't work that way.

I understand there's an interesting story behind the way you met your wife that ties in with your activism. Would you like to share that?

We met online. She was in a group called Christian Forums, and I found myself there arguing with religious believers online. And I ended up in an argument with her. I made the challenge that I often make, that I can prove evolution to your satisfaction. It's a Socratic method. I don't have a specific set of questions or anything. I just feel out where you are on this topic and then start asking you questions to direct you to what reality is. What usually happens is that people refuse the challenge altogether. On the rare occasion that anyone has accepted that challenge, they bolt when they realize that it is effective. It gets them to understand what they don't want to believe. And that's what they're really afraid of. They want to believe what they already know can't really be true. But as I said, that's not everyone. There are people who believe as they do because they've been deceived, and they're like, if most of the planet believes this, then there must be some truth to it.

My wife happened to be one of these. She was the only person who ever took that challenge all the way to the end, and she eventually conceded that evolution was an actual thing. It's real. It's not a belief. It's something you can actually prove to people. When she admitted in her community—she lived in a small town in Texas—that she no longer believed in Creationism, she was ostracized by the entire community.

Now when you come up and tell me that you're an atheist and now you're a Creationist, I'm sure as hell going to want to ask you a bunch of questions. I'm going to want to know what went wrong in your head that you're thinking this. What did somebody tell you that convinced you of that? But religious believers don't do that, and the answer for this is obvious: they don't want to know what changed your mind. Because they don't want their minds changed. That's why I said it's all make believe.

MANDISA THOMAS

Mandisa Thomas grew up in the early 1980s in Fayetteville, Georgia, in the home of a non-religious single parent. However, she says her grandmother was a devout Christian. As a result, Thomas sometimes attended church, even singing in the choir. She realized she was an atheist at a young age and has long been interested in the historical ties between Christianity and the Black community. She came to realize that Christianity had been ingrained into the Black identity in America by force. Although she realized this at a relatively young age, she quickly discovered that many members of the Black community saw such suggestions and observations as a form of betrayal. This was a verboten topic for most Black people in America.

Hoping to expand the conversation about the effects religion has had on the Black identity, she eventually established Black Nonbelievers, Inc. in Atlanta in 2011, where she currently serves as the non-profit organization's president. In subsequent years, Black Nonbelievers, Inc. has branched out significantly, and now has local chapters in ten U.S. cities.

In 2012, Thomas was featured on a prominently placed Atlanta billboard next to Langston Hughes as part of a campaign sponsored by African Americans for Humanism. Thomas has spoken at numerous secular events and in 2013 she, along with Ayanna Watson, established the Blackout Secular Rally in New York City. Thomas has been featured on numerous radio shows and podcasts, and has been a special contributor to CNN, where she has spoken frequently on the struggles of being a Black atheist in America and the relationship between religion and the struggles of the Black community.

The interview as presented here is a combination of two separate interviews with Thomas, which were conducted in 2016 and 2018.

* * *

Did you grow up in a religious household?

Not per se. I did grow up around a lot of religious people, but my household in particular wasn't really religious. And that's kind of rare in my community. I wasn't raised religious. I wasn't made to go to church or made to believe in god every Sunday. I sang in various churches growing up, under a voice instructor, so I do have some exposure to the church and to religion. But I was never forced to go to church. My mother would let me go to church with my very religious grandmother if I wanted to, but it was not a requirement. I wasn't forced to go to Bible study or anything like that.

At what age did you begin to question the value of religion?

Part of my upbringing was being raised in what is called the Black consciousness community, in which we learned a lot about Black history and culture growing up. I actually learned early on how Christianity in particular was forced upon the African captives when they were enslaved here in the United States. I also read a lot of mythology growing up; I was exposed to some African mythology, as well as Greek and Roman mythology. So when I listened to people preach or I listened to religious folks in churches and sort of halfway paid attention to the sermon, I would try to make the distinction and differentiate between the gods and I wondered why it was that the Christian god was so prevalent, and why does he seem more scary than the others? [Laughs.] So I would say I was about eight or nine when I started questioning religion and the god concept.

Did you voice that questioning to anyone?
Not really. I remember having a disagreement with a religious cousin of mine when we were teenagers. She said we were all born in sin, and I said, "That doesn't make any sense, logically. Babies are born innocent. They don't know anything. How can they be born in sin?" I was just asking that question from a logical perspective, because that statement made no sense to me whatsoever. I was like, "That just sounds ridiculous." [Laughs again.] I was more vocal about issues pertaining to the Black community, like systemic racism and injustice, more than anything else. Religion just didn't come up too much.

I remember when I was in high school someone asked me if I was an atheist, and I didn't know what that meant. They said it meant I didn't believe in heaven or hell, and when I thought about it I thought, that kind of makes sense. I had already started questioning heaven and hell and thinking about death at an early age. I could just never reconcile the idea of a heaven because there was no evidence. I wondered about what happened when we die, and it was a scary prospect. I mean, no one had ever come back from the dead. I remember lying in bed at night thinking about it and thinking, I'm just going to try to live the best life that I can until that happens. I tried to believe in the concept of heaven and hell, because it would keep coming up, but again, no one has ever come back from the dead to say there's a heaven or hell. So I just continued to think about that over the years. I never really asked anyone, but I remember attending funerals growing up and I looked at the bodies and I just couldn't really say they were in heaven. That concept was just never put into my head that a god existed or that a heaven or hell existed and I had to believe I was going there when I died. So yeah, that would come up in thought when I was young.

I know that you are a parent, and I always try to ask atheist parents this question—how do you approach raising your children in regards to religion?

My daughter is eighteen-years-old, and she identifies as atheist. Her father and I taught her about various religions; we taught her that people believe in different things, but that we don't believe in them. My boys, who are seven and ten., we've explained to them that there are different beliefs out there. They are well aware of my activism within the secular community. They are well aware that we are atheist nonbelievers. I don't really talk to them about religion too much—we just try to be normal parents. We may be a little less strict when it comes to what they watch or read. We give them guidance, but we think it's a bad idea to shelter them from what they will eventually grow up to see anyway. We've always kept things open and objective with them. My son Isiah said, "Mom, do you believe in god?" I said, "You know I don't," and he said, "Well, I believe in god." So I said, "Which one?" He couldn't really answer that, so I said, "It's okay if you do, but you need to have a good reason why." He was seven or eight at the time, so I didn't really push it with him.

We try not to expose them to too much of the religious teachings because a lot of it is really, really horrible. A lot of those stories in the Bible are just really bad. [Laughs.] I don't want to force them to read any of that, because it's just so horrible. So I try to keep them away from it as much as possible until they get to an age where they can better understand some of the content. If they want to know more about it, we won't shy away from the subject. But until then, we just keep it away from them.

The fear is that if you don't indoctrinate your children, then someone else will try to.

Indoctrination comes in many forms, not just religion. There are cultural and traditional indoctrinations—things that are passed down from generation to generation, which is another problem in the Black community. Religion and tradition get kind of lumped into the same thing. I've been fortunate with my in-laws. I think my mother-in-law tried that one time, where she asked my kids if they had ever heard of god and she told them that one day she would tell them about him. I told her, "No, you're not!" [Laughs.] I was very adamant about that. Since then, we've actually had some good conversations about questioning faith. They're actually very supportive of how we've raised our children. They don't try to indoctrinate them. They don't say much about religion to them, at least not that I'm aware of. But my boys are so very outspoken that they would tell us about it anyway!

We're raising them to question everything. We're raising them to be skeptics and critical thinkers. We've taught them that if something doesn't feel right, you question it and you challenge it. Not to be disrespectful of other people's beliefs, but if something doesn't make sense in terms of logic, we've taught them they have the right to stand up and say, "This sounds like crap." [Chuckles.] I think they do a very good job of that.

So I try to remember that religion isn't the only form of indoctrination. I didn't escape indoctrination. I was raised to believe that all white people were evil based on our history and what has happened to us as a people. But I've tried to unlearn that and take it on a case-by-case basis while still acknowledging the collective responsibility of the white race and what has happened throughout time. But I realized I couldn't hold that against every white individual. There are forms of indoctrination, whether we realize it or not, that aren't religion based.

You founded Black Nonbelievers, Inc. Please tell me about that.
We are a secular fellowship that is dedicated to increasing the visibility of Black atheists and those who are non-religious. We build communities, as well. We hold events that bring people together. We're not exclusive to the Black community. Our main objective is to show that there are atheists within the Black community in a secular community that seems to be overwhelmingly white or represented by whites. And you have a Black community that is very much religiously identified, so there is a notion, even in the Black community, that there are no Black nonbelievers. "We don't have atheists. Atheism is a white thing. White folks can be atheist, but Black folks can't possibly be atheist." Or if we are, then we're seen as betraying our community. So the primary purpose is for us to show that

we do exist, and for those atheists in our community who have felt isolated for so long and deal with so much pressure from religious family and friends to be able to see that there are others out there like them who go through the same struggles. That spawned the need for Black Nonbelievers—to build a bridge between folks in the Black community and the secular community.

Have you received much opposition?

Not much. We've received more support than opposition. But there has been some opposition from Blacks who are very religious, as well as from some white folks who believe we're being separatists or trying to separate by race. Before they even look at our website to find out what we're all about, they see the word "Black" on it and they get offended. "Well, what if there was a White Nonbelievers?" But there are other groups targeted towards certain demographics because there are needs to those demographics that they can personally understand. Therefore, we are no different. To say that we're being separatists is a ridiculous notion—especially when you don't try to find out what it is that we're actually about. So yes, we have received some opposition, but we've received more support than anything else.

In 2013, Ayanna Watson and yourself established the Blackout Secular Rally in Queens, New York. Tell me about that.

It was a celebration of the diversity and how far Black atheists and Black nonbelievers have come, not just as organizations, but also as a demographic. We've seen more people come out and openly identify as atheists. We've been able to actually build those connections and establish those avenues where people can connect in a better way. There's also a tremendous amount of literary and creative talent within the Black secular community that we knew existed and we decided to showcase. Within the white community, you have your Richard Dawkins, and your Christopher Hitchens, and Sam Harris... You have other scholars who are highly-regarded and rightfully so, but we wanted to show that there are other writers and talent that tends to be overlooked. And we've been able to showcase them. For instance, you have Jeremiah Camara who produced the documentary *Contradiction*, which spoke to the issues of the church within the Black community. We have showcased authors who have compiled anthologies, some who have written about their own personal journeys and have chronicled the Black atheist experience. So the Blackout rally was a celebration of that, but it was also a celebration of our establishing ourselves within the secular community. We have allies in the other organizations who understand what our missions are. They understand that we need each other's help in order to push our missions forward for the betterment of everyone.

As you've stated in the past, belief in god has become a "fixation" within the Black community. Why do you feel that is, and how can it be overcome?

I've actually compared it to a crutch. It has become a crutch, and it is a fixation, because of slavery. At a time when it was illegal to teach slaves to read and write, the only thing that many Blacks had going for them was their faith. At a time after slavery and reconstruction in particular, when the Jim Crow laws were put into place and Blacks were effectively disenfranchised from the United States, the church was one of the only institutions that Blacks had where they could have a sense of support in their community. For some people, that just became everything for them. The church was everything at a time when we had nothing. So now, because of the emotional attachment to music, and the way the pastors were revered in churches, the prominence that is placed on church has just carried over as a tradition. It's to the point where now people are holding on to it and using it to replace the need for information. People are forgetting that times have changed and that church has become a big business that banks on people's faith and loyalty. They're banking on the loyalty and influence it's had on the community for such a long time, that it has become a fixation and it has become a crutch because people have become too dependent on it. Instead of using measures that have been scientifically proven to help our community, many people are still relying on the church as an end-all, be-all. It is beginning to change, but the historical aspect plays a huge role in why it's still a fixation in our community.

Are you seeing a growth of atheism within the Black community right now?

There is definitely growth within the Black community, although the number of religious households is still pretty high. I recently completed an interview with NPR and the latest numbers are at 87 percent of Black households who are still religious. I'm hoping in the near future, with more people finding our organization and more people openly identifying, that those numbers will decrease. But there does seem to be a shift in the number of people who are more open about their nonbelief and their atheism. So it is growing. I do see that there are also more Black folks who are at least open to talking about religion and the problems that they have with religion. So even if they don't openly identify, there are certainly more people who are open to expressing their criticism of religion and church.

I've heard that there is a lot of sexism and, quite frankly, racism within the atheist community. Have you experienced much of those things?

I most certainly have. As one of the leaders in the secular community, I do find that sometimes my points may be overlooked in favor of a man—especially a degreed white male. Sometimes that does play a part. I have been seen as not being able to run an organization as a woman. That has come up. Luckily it doesn't come up too often, but it has come up before. There is some sexism and some racism. I've experienced that, as well. Because of the faces that are widely regarded within the secular community, we still tend to be overlooked. And these are some of the same people who wonder how they can attract more people of color—"How can we achieve this diversity that we say we want?"—and it becomes more of a talking point. Nobody actually wants to do anything about it. We get asked certain questions that seem to be very oblivious—just unrelateable questions—by those who are academically inclined but have hardly any common sense. Sometimes we're seen as being aliens, if you will. We don't go through the same things as they do. Sometimes Black atheists are seen as an afterthought. People say they don't see color and that we should all just be one community, and we are, but many tend to ignore some of the specific issues that we deal with as people of color. That does tend to be dismissed in favor of only wanting to focus on the science aspect or the critical thinking aspect, and that may not be the focus of someone who is dealing with certain factors that come from our specific community.

. . .

There aren't many people of color at the more broad, mainstream atheist events. Are there things that organizers should be doing or changing in their approach in an effort to attract more people of color? What are some things they could be doing that they currently are not doing?

I always try to be conscious of being the token black speaker at these events. I appreciate that the organizers like what I have to say and that I offer something of value. I am often asked about speaker recommendations... I think that there's a focus on the celebrity atheists; the big name atheists who draw in crowds, if you will. While I don't see anything wrong with meeting a demand if there is one, I do think there are more of us out there, Black atheist women and younger people, who are out there that they could be reaching out to. They shouldn't be totally relying on someone like me to refer them to them. I think it would be good for them to do some research on the atheist speakers of color who are out there. There are quite a few of us.

Also, we just held our first ever Convention at Sea last year, and we're also doing that again this year. We welcome everyone at our event. So if they would like to know more about the speakers that come from our community, they can certainly tap into our events. They should definitely be doing their research and doing more due diligence. I can say organizations like the Secular Student Alliance and American Atheists have been increasing their lineup to include more speakers of color and more women. They've been answering that call, but there's still more work to be done there.

You mentioned your Convention at Sea and that you're gearing up to have another one. What can you tell me about that? What does that entail?

The first Convention at Sea was held aboard the Carnival Sensation. It sailed out of Miami, and we will be doing that again. One thing we like to do at Black Nonbelievers is to incorporate fun with the community building and support, as well as hearing some fantastic speakers and getting to meet them. What we did, we organized a five-day cruise and we had talks and sessions on the ship. We also organized events around what's already on the ship, like for example the karaoke and the shore excursion. That gives people the chance to get to know one another, to network and get to know the speakers before and during their presentations. So it isn't all just sitting on the ship and having a convention all day long. It's a mixture of fun and information and networking and community.

It was a great experience and gave an opportunity to those who weren't aware of us to see us gather as a group so they know there is an organized effort there.

You are an atheist. You're Black. You're a woman. I hate to bring politics into this, but with this particular administration, a lot of those things come into play and are affected. It seems like Donald Trump has changed what it means to be an activist in general. Has this administration changed what you do?

The issues that we face have been ongoing for a while, but what we've seen happen, what we've seen shift, are the organizations that we are now able to work with as a result of this administration. For example, in the Atlanta area the organizers for the Women's March reached out to us to be community partners and we were also a sponsor for their anniversary event. We have more common goals now as far as women and people of color as a marginalized community. I think it's bringing more people together more than ever to speak out against this administration and the things that are taking place. I think more people are realizing that we have a lot more in common that we're fighting for than we realized. It's affecting all of us.

I think that's a good shift. I hate that it took this administration to bring that out, but I'm finding that now it's becoming more prudent and more important that people speak out. There's a lot we have to be concerned about with this administration and with the policies that are being put in place that will affect all of us, believers and nonbelievers alike. I think now it has become more of a human thing to become concerned about than our differences in religious ideology or religious perspective.

As evangelicals start to seize our educational system a little more every day, it scares me as it assures that students are not going to be encouraged to analyze scientific findings and theories that may stand in opposition to the Bible. Is this something that concerns you, and in your opinion, where can we go from here?

I'm actually glad that now as I take on activism full time I'm able to look out for these things more and also speak out on them more. It is important for us to become involved as much as we can—writing letters to our representatives, attending school board meetings and to speak up when we see something that is very crucial. It can be very difficult at times. It can be very difficult, period. But it is important to get involved. The power really does start locally with what we get involved in. So now I have a great opportunity to become more involved and more outspoken as an atheist and to help people see that we are here and this is an organized effort. I can encourage more people to get involved with the local process to affect change, because it won't change until we get more involved. There's a lot to unpack there. It starts on the local level. We have to get more involved there. It doesn't just start and end with the presidency or the national election. It starts locally, and activism takes on many forms. If you can support the people who are out there on the front lines and behind the scenes, there's a lot that can be done collectively. I think when we start rethinking what activism is and what we can do, then things will start to change.

Of all the things that you do in your activism, what is your favorite thing that you do? What is the aspect of your work that you enjoy the most?

I enjoy the tabling and the outreach. I also enjoy our meetings where people are meeting us for the first time; they thought they were the only ones out there. Actually engaging people. At the anniversary event of the Women's March there were other black women there who were like, "Wow!" Some were very intrigued, but others were like, "Oh my gosh, I thought I was the only one. I'm glad to see you here." So I think being visible and having people seeing us, whether we are tabling or we are hosting another event, has become my favorite part. It's because that's when we start dispelling the misconceptions about atheism and what atheists look like and who we are. That's been my favorite part about being active in this movement—for people to really see us and engage us. Not only do they see that there are more of us, but I think if they never met an atheist before it's important that they had a good experience.

That's true. I think sometimes some of the people who are out there visibly representing the atheist community don't always represent us in the best ways. I can see how seeing them might leave people with the impression that all atheists are pushy, closed-minded people. I mean, there are some of every kind of person in every group. But mostly we're...we're just people.

[Laughs.] But a lot of people think we worship the devil and probably bite the heads off babies.

Yeah. I would say that there are some atheists whom I certainly don't... I don't take credit for all atheists. There are some atheist jerks out there. Unfortunately there are some who are showing themselves to be jerks more and more. The one thing I'm finding is that just because you're an atheist doesn't necessarily make you more logical or rational than a believer, which is unfortunate because I do hold us to that higher expectation.

I used to believe that was going to be the case, but it isn't always. I sometimes think, you were able to get from here to here and make this logical jump regarding religion, so why do you then have these backwards beliefs? It's disheartening sometimes.

I think it's still the responsibility of the believer to look beyond their own perspectives and to understand that not everyone does share the same point of view. Also, we must be careful that even though we represent a marginalized community as atheists, we can't speak for all atheists. And we don't have to apologize for them. Also, there's so much good work being done within the community that I would hate for us to be scared off by the ones who don't represent us well. If there are some that you see aren't the best; there are more of us out here. While it can be a bit disheartening, we are people. We don't have to accept all things that human beings do. We continue to move forward. Not just move on, but move forward. I think the worst thing we can do is to deny that we're capable of doing bad things. But I do think there are more of us doing good than not. I don't think we need to defend those things, but I think it is important to acknowledge that part.

JOZEF K. RICHARDS

Jozef K. Richards is a Milwaukee-based filmmaker and founder and owner of King's Tower Productions, which distributes media through Amazon and YouTube. In 2011, he made his feature film debut with *The Amateur Monster Movie*. He directed his second film, *The Wayward Sun*, the following year. He is writer and producer of the religious satire series *Holy Shit*, which "takes aim at religious dogma, its lack of credibility, and pokes fun at the lesser-known absurdities of the Bible and similar religious texts, including many of those taken literally by some sects of the Christian faith." The show often features skits starring atheist scholars and celebrity guests.

In 2015, Richards began work on a documentary titled *Batman & Jesus*. The film, made in association with Mythicist Milwaukee, introduces the evidence both for and against the existence of Jesus. The film, which debuted on September 30, 2017 at Milwaukee's Pabst Theater, included research, interviews, and vetting from numerous scholars, authors, historians, and popular secular voices including Dr. Robert M. Price, Dr.

Richard Carrier, David Fitzgerald, Faisal Saeed Al Mutar, Allie Jackson, and hip-hop artist Killah Priest. The teaser trailer for the film debuted during the Reason Rally in 2016, where it played as the lead-in video for a Wu-Tang Clan concert.

* * *

Tell me about your background in regards to religion. Do you come from a religious home?

I was Catholic growing up. My family on both my mother and father's sides were Catholic. I attended a Catholic grade school until I was in the sixth grade. A lot of my childhood was at a Catholic school, and then I stopped going. At that point, my family stopped attending church. They stopped going because they felt the community was sort of fake—people would act a certain way during the week and then think they'd be forgiven on Sunday so they could carry on. They just got tired of that.

I was 12 at the time, and I was fairly indoctrinated by the Catholic school. I thought, "I can't stop going to church or I'll go to hell. I have to keep going." So I started riding my bike to church, and at that point, being that I was now going on my own accord, I started paying more attention. I was hearing things I had heard a dozen times before—they would repeat the same passages on the same days every year. I realized I had questions about many of the things they were telling me, such as the Trinity and "just what is the Holy Spirit?" I quickly found that they couldn't really answer my questions, whether it was a priest or my Sunday school teacher. I got a lot of "that's a mystery"-type of answers. So I thought I would read the Bible myself to see what was in there. Surely in those hundreds of pages this book would answer my questions. And it didn't. What it did tell me was that it was all sort of absurd. Even at that age I thought it was absurd. I got as far as Noah's ark and I just couldn't believe any of it. At that point I guess I became an agnostic.

Since then I have declared myself an atheist, but yeah, my childhood was Catholic. I dove into it all pretty deep and finally decided it didn't make any sense to me.

At what age did you start making films?

Those times sort of lined up. I had always written stories and plays and comics and drawings, ever since I was a small child. So that was sort of a lifelong interest of mine, but as far as making them into a movie, it wasn't until I was about 12, which was pretty much the same time period where I stopped going to church. My friend had a video camera. He said, "Come over. A bunch of us are going to make a movie with my camera." So I went over to his house and enjoyed that, and at the end of the day I said, "I write all these stories and plays. Why don't we turn that into a movie?" Since then, I've been relentlessly doing that. More or less, my whole life has been about telling stories.

Your documentary Batman & Jesus *has a rather interesting angle. Please talk about that?*

I came into contact with this group from Milwaukee called Mythicist Milwaukee. A family friend approached me because they were interested in making a documentary. So I went to hear what they had in mind. They basically just wanted to make a documentary that improved on the scholarship of *Zeitgeist*. And they said they would be able to get a budget. Since they didn't really have much of an idea, I went home and worked on some ideas myself. I was just sort of writing down eye-catching titles, I guess. It was just sort of whatever came to my mind. I was writing down things like *Oh, My God* or *Holy Shit*—stuff like that. Then for some reason I thought of *Batman & Jesus*. I don't know why I wrote that down, but as soon as I did I started thinking about what that might be.

These guys didn't just want to remake *Zeitgeist*. They had more information because they had been turned on to these scholars like Richard Carrier, Robert Price, and David Fitzgerald, whom you might call mythicists. They had a mythicist perspective. I wasn't very knowledgeable about that. I had seen *Zeitgeist* and I had seen *The God Who Wasn't There*. I had opinions of my own. But I wasn't really familiar with the word "mythicist," which is the idea that religion is based in myth rather than fact. This sort of introduced the idea to me that Jesus may have been a myth.

And while I already considered the story of Jesus to be a myth, it had never occurred to me that the person Jesus was also a myth. I always assumed that he was a real person. Anything I had ever read in history class or on television, always seemed to be written with the assumption that this was a real person. It never occurred to me that he wasn't. But when I listened to some of their lectures and read things they had written and listened to them debate and speak on the subject, I realized that there really wasn't much evidence at all that Jesus was a real person. All of the so-called evidence came from the book that I considered to be a myth. This was a big moment for me. I had never thought of it that way, but I couldn't form an argument that this was a real person. At the very least I have to say that I do not know; I have to be agnostic about whether or not this was a real person.

Suddenly I had another a-ha! moment with the title *Batman & Jesus*, which I thought was very striking. It sounds controversial and it wasn't two names you were used to seeing together. It immediately gets your attention, which is what I wanted the title to do. But could I actually make a film behind this? So the approach is that Batman is a myth, as well. We know this because it's modern and the history is readily available. There are people alive today who were alive when Batman was created. But it has a lot of messages in it and its meanings change over time. Suddenly, all these parallels between Jesus and Batman started to come together for me. Jesus was also written by many different authors over a long period of time, with different versions and deviations that sort of made sense within the culture of the time.

So the movie is comparing the evolution of this archetype. I'm not comparing how similar the characters are. I mean, Superman would be more similar to Jesus in that respect. But the comparison is more so in the architecture of how this character came to be and how it grew into having such a large following. I think Batman and Jesus are two of the most well known characters in the world. You could go almost anywhere in the world and people would know each of them. There really aren't too many other characters you could say that about.

You have some interesting people involved with the film. Tell me about the people you've got in it and how you went about getting some of them.

I first started doing this in April of 2015. Robert Price, Richard Carrier, David Fitzgerald...these were people who sort of turned me on to this information. These were also people that Mythicist Milwaukee was approaching for interviews and lining up for conferences they were holding. Knowing that they were coming to town, I said, "Let's interview them in the movie." And the first conference that took place once I linked up with this group was with David Fitzgerald and Killah Priest, who is a Wu-Tang Clan affiliate. I said, "Let's get him into the movie, too." I'm a fan of the Wu-Tang Clan's music and even though he's not a scholar, I thought, let's get some other people in here that are interesting to people in a different way. They were both willing to be in it. It was pretty simple. They also did a skit on a show I do called *Holy Shit*, which was one of the first titles I came up with when I was first approached to do this film. And they were really cool.

Then Richard Carrier came to town and we recorded with him. And then what happened was, there's this event called Reason Rally. Killah Priest was connected with us from the documentary and from coming to this conference, so we became sort of networked with the people running Reason Rally. We talked to Killah Priest about getting other acts from Wu-Tang to perform. With Killah Priest's help, we ended up lining up most of the key members of Wu-Tang Clan. They agreed to perform at Reason Rally. Because we were sort of tied to that, they agreed to play the trailer for *Batman & Jesus* before their performance. So that was great. It was very cool meeting these guys. I only got to meet most of them very briefly, but it was very cool to talk to them. The other people who were at Reason Rally—people like Bill Nye and Penn Jillette and Paul Provenza—were great, too. I kept seeing Paul Provenza all day because I had access to the green room where all of the guests were. I was able to chat with him quite a bit. I then chatted with him at some of the other events after the rally. Ultimately he said he would like to be a part of the movie, and very generously agreed to come film with us for free. He recorded some narration for the movie, and he recorded some skits with us. He was really one of the nicest people. No complaints. Lots of fun. He's also a very well connected person whose involvement with the project was very big.

I interviewed Aron Ra. He was really great. He had lots of

great stories. He's also very intelligent and has a huge wealth of knowledge. He's really more of a showman than some of these straight-up scholars. Aron Ra is a lot more dramatic than they are. He brought a lot of flavor to things.

When you debuted the trailer for the film at Reason Rally, what kinds of reactions did you receive?

Well, they didn't introduce it. They just started playing it, and I don't know for sure if it was in the program. But I think at first people were sort of like, "What is this? I'm a little bit confused." As it kept going, the reaction seemed to be, "Is this really a movie, or is this a joke?" Then when we're in the Bat church and he's singing the Batman theme, and everybody started to laugh. Then people started to get intrigued. We heard from a lot of people and we got a lot of great feedback on it. I think that's probably the reaction from a lot of people—confusion, followed by laughter, followed by intrigue. [Laughs.] I think that will probably be the reaction to the movie as a whole.

Tell me about the Amazon series Holy Shit, *which you produce and appear on.*

Holy Shit is a web series that I make. I started making it in 2015, shortly after I started working on *Batman & Jesus*. The reason I started doing it was to begin to build some credibility of my own in the atheist community, to sort of gain some momentum going into *Batman & Jesus*. I wanted to make something I could be self-reliant upon. Out of everything I've ever made, it's probably the one thing I've had my hands in just about every aspect of, from writing to performing to directing and editing. I can do it mostly by myself.

The show is that I count down absurd things in the Bible in a humorous, satirical way. Then we have cutaways to humorous skits to sort of emphasize some of the points that I'm making. We've done the "Top 10 Commandments in the Bible," where I break down the commandments. I picked out what I believed to be 10 that were silly or offensive and made them into a list. I've done "Top 10 Fantasy Creatures." "Top 10 Killers." "Top 10 Christmas Traditions That Didn't Originate With Christianity." The show is really sort of me highlighting absurd things about our religious practices that are not necessarily at the forefront of peoples' minds. It's all in the Bible. I don't use other sources. I'm purely just going off the Bible, with the exception of the Christmas episode. It's fairly surprising information if you're not aware of it.

Working on those are a lot of fun. I wish I could do more, but they're just very time consuming.

Just for shits and giggles, if Batman and Jesus were to do battle, who would win and why?

[Laughs.] I haven't thought of this before. I think that as intelligent as he may be, and as resourceful and wealthy as he may be, can Batman really compete with immortality and legions of angels that will come to do Jesus' bidding? Much like Superman, Jesus is very overpowering, although I hear Batman more or less wins against Superman in the movie, so maybe there's a way Batman can defeat Jesus. [Laughs again.] I don't know what he would have to do to beat Jesus, but assuming they were both real and fighting, I have a hard time coming up with a way that Batman could defeat Jesus.

DAVE MCKEAN

Born in 1963, Dave McKean is an accomplished artist working in a number of different fields, from illustrations, painting, photography, collage, digital art, to sculpture. He has worked on such noted comic books as *Hellblazer*, *Arkham Asylum: A Serious House on Serious Earth*, and produced the covers for many of Neil Gaiman's celebrated *Sandman* comics. Of McKean, Gaiman once wrote, "People ask me who my favorite artist is to work with. I've worked with world-class artists, after all, heaps of them. World-class people. And when they ask me about my favorite, I say Dave McKean. And then people ask why. I say, because he surprises me." McKean's artwork is so distinctive and recognizable that art directors sometimes assign their artists to work in a "Dave McKean style." McKean illustrated the cover for Stephen King's *Dark Tower IV: Wizard and Glass*, designed album covers for musical artists as varied as Alice Cooper and Counting Crows, and even done some film directing for a number of projects (including *MirrorMask*, which he co-wrote with Gaiman). He is an accomplished author in his own right.

In 2011, McKean teamed up with noted atheist writer Richard Dawkins to produce a children's book titled, *The Magic of Reality: How We Know What's Really True*. In his review for *The Guardian*, critic Tim Radford praised the book as being "prodigiously illustrated and beautifully designed." He went on to say the book was a "distillation of so much that Dawkins has written and argued.... The strength is that he knows his ground. The weakness is that—for a 'family audience'—he deliberately constrains his vocabulary along with the exuberant imagery and belligerence that made his reputation from the start."

* * *

When did you first begin to question religion?

Religious belief of any kind was never really part of my childhood. My mother vaguely believes in something, but she's not really sure what. My father died when I was young, and used to call Christianity "the grumblings of old men."

I don't remember ever taking any of it literally, and once I had any sense of the history of religion, it seemed so obviously a means for the powerful to control the flock, I lost any deference I might have had as a child.

But, I've always been fascinated with the need we have to believe in something, the need for a purpose in life, something to give what we do value. One of the first books I bought was a collection of creation myths from various cultures. The imagery was wonderfully imaginative, and betrayed so much of how people think, how their particular stories are embedded in their surroundings, climate, and social structures. And I've always been interested in the Bible as a series of stories. After spending a year with Richard on this book, the day after finishing it, I went to Port Talbot to start a year's work with Michael Sheen making a film version of his *Passion of Port Talbot*, a secular retelling of the Easter story. Seeing 20,000 people surrounding a roundabout in a small Welsh town to watch a man be crucified in the year 2011 was very strange, and rather wonderful. It re-affirmed for me that all these things—stories, theatre, religion, culture—are all essentially about human connection, experiencing something powerful together.

How did this collaboration between Richard Dawkins and yourself come about?

I have been an admirer of Richard's books and lectures for a long time, and I read several times in interviews that he was considering writing a book for children. I've illustrated several children's books, and I thought this was a great idea, but it didn't seem to be appearing. So I wondered if I could put my name up for consideration if the book was still being planned. I asked my agent Merrilee Heiftez to find out who I needed to talk to, and it turned out to be a wonderful chap called John Brockman, who is agent to all the star science writers, ex-gallarist and friend of Warhol and John Cale, whom I've worked with, and editor of The Edge website. I met John in London, he was keen, and passed my work on to Richard. We met at Richard's place in Oxford and it turned out that the book hadn't got very far at all. There were three or four sketched out possibilities, but nothing had been received very enthusiastically by Richard's publisher. But one of the ideas really intrigued me—a series of questions, answered initially with myths, folk stories, and theological stories, and then answered with our very best scientific explanations. This seemed to be perfect for an illustrated book, allowing plenty of imaginative interpretations in the myth sections, and then the chance, and challenge, of making the science sections even more wondrous and engaging, both with the clarity of Richard's writing and using every tool in my illustration box of tricks. Richard wrote a sample chapter "What is a Rainbow?" and I illustrated it. John Brockman took it out to market, and we were off.

What was the collaborative process like between Richard and yourself?

It became obvious very early on that we would have to closely plan out each chapter, especially the science sections, as they had to be technically correct. It was also obvious that my natural tendency towards a more symbolic or poetic approach to imagery wasn't going to work so well here. I didn't want the book just to be full of diagrams and maps, so I tried to find interesting, amusing, and atmospheric visual ideas throughout. I was very keen that every page be illustrated, that the whole experience be visual. I don't believe Richard's ideas *need* illustrating, but part of the initial part of doing the book was to reach out to new readers, maybe children and adults who wouldn't usually read Richard's work or even open a science book, but may be drawn in by the visuals. So the pictures had a few different jobs to do, hopefully not sending mixed signals and certainly not getting in the way of the text. It was a balancing act. I think we found a good rhythm by about half way through.

I responded to each chapter and worked out some roughs, then I produced doodle roughs for the myth sections, as they were not so factually important, and then more finished visuals for the science sections. We had to consult specialists on occasions—a noted immunologist, Carolyn Porco who worked on the Cassini mission—and for a couple of chapters I talked to my children's teachers at school to help me with the Periodic Table and *experimentum crucis*. We then had a meeting to discuss my ideas and then I got on with the final illustration. I suggested layouts throughout, as I always like the design of my books to be bound into the imagery.

Why do you feel a book like The Magic of Reality *is important in the dialogue with young people?*

One thing that really mystifies me is the false division that often seems to exist between the scientific view of life, and other ways of thinking about the world. Science is often seen as literal, reductive, obsessed with explaining the mechanics of things, and not able to deal with the magic, mystery, art, and imaginative aspects of life. Whereas, like Richard Feynman's famous example of the workings of a flower, I think understanding the science behind everything only expands, broadens, and deepens the wonder.

Since there are so many children's books retelling Bible stories and Greek myths and other fantastical fare, I think it's very important to try and redress the balance a little, especially now. We seem to be living through a very confusing time. The Internet offers so much information but so little knowledge, so many stories but so few compelling storytellers, so much opinion and so few facts by comparison. People often have a very slippery, and sometimes rather negative idea of the scientific truths we have discovered. Everything is 'relative.' Well, science certainly doesn't know everything, but it knows a hell of a lot, and the solid foundations of our knowledge in so many areas are what mankind will need in the future if we are going to navigate the difficulties we face ahead. Science has something to say about absolutely everything in our lives, and it's important to encourage that curiosity at as young an age as possible.

. . .

What aspects of the book are you the most proud of?

I'm very proud to have done it. As a parent of two, I hope my wife and I have brought them up in an open-minded environment, and encouraged them to question and think for themselves. To understand the arguments in all fields, so that they can see how they are connected, and see how new information confirms or contradicts the views they currently have. So to have contributed to a book that I believe does just that, is very gratifying, and has influenced the kinds of projects I've been keen to do since then. I'm happy with most of the imagery. I think we could have gone a lot further with design and the kinds of game playing and storytelling you can achieve when words and pictures work well with each other, but it was always Richard's book and he had to be comfortable with the visual component—something he's never had to deal with before. I'm happy that the book has been translated into so many languages and has traveled around the world so successfully.

One thing I really appreciated about the book is that, rather than taking aim at Judeo-Christianity, as many atheist books do, you guys instead looked at many different religions and treated them all equally.

I'm certainly much more interested in questioning the faith-based way of thinking, rather than taking aim at any one religion or belief. They are all fundamentally the same, I think, in that they are based on teachings from a book or elder, unsupported by evidence, with faith as their supporting structure. Faith, and the various punishments threatened on you—socially while you're alive, and eternally once you're dead—keep the whole religious train on its narrow tracks. The scientific view, that every claim needs to be tested and supported by repeatable evidence, seems to me to be the only way to deal with everything in life, from political points of view to the very innermost feelings we have about why we're here and how we should spend our handful of years alive. I've changed my mind about many things over the years, as new evidence is discovered, or better arguments made, and although I have a strong foundation culled from my family background, my friends, my experience, I've tried to remain non-dogmatic about everything—it's a balance. So, regarding this book, I think we both wanted to tackle the mindset rather than people's specific faith choices. To be honest, I tend to feel people's individual private beliefs are none of my business. We all create a view of the world, our own gods to a degree. Some are formed within an established church. Mine wasn't, but if I had to identify my god in some form, I would call it creativity. Art has no obvious function; I choose to believe that it's crucial to our species in keeping our brains nourished. Creative thought has many other uses, but art in its purest, most abstract form (music for example), simply keeps our minds fit, in the same way that food, energy, and physical exercise keeps our bodies fit.

What kinds of feedback have you received from parents?

I'm sure I've only had feedback from a rather narrow group of parents. I think you're already sympathetic to the cause if you've bought the book and encouraged your children to read it. I've had some good feedback from children and adults about both the way it's presented and the ideas in the text. To a degree you feel like you are preaching to the converted, and I'm not sure how to get beyond that. I suppose I hope that amongst the many adults and children who are still sitting on the fence

—rational enough to see the truth in the scientific method, but unable to completely let go of superstition or the social pressures and comforts of belief—then maybe the book will be one more chip on the table in favor of the enlightenment. From my point of view as an artist, or illustrator, I hope the book helps to erase the line that often exists between rational science and imaginative art. I think right now, and it's probably always been the case, science needs the influence of art to think of irrational possibilities, to disturb dogmatic thinking, and to connect with those deep emotional needs we have. And art needs the influence of science to add truth and reality to what we do, to show us the vast and awe-inspiring raw material of the universe from which we can interpret and express new ideas.

Will we ever see another Richard Dawkins/Dave McKean collaboration?

Well, I would love to do another project with Richard, any time. Unfortunately, I had a very rough time with the publisher of this book, so I doubt it would be another book unless it was with a different publisher.

What types of problems did you have with the publisher?

I feel the publisher didn't really *get* it. They had a very templated, dreary view of how a book should be designed and how it should read. The art department didn't know what it wanted until they saw it, so as a rule they do fifty or sixty cover roughs, all to almost finished standard, which means they are mostly cutting and pasting from the Internet. They show proposals to book buyers and then allow them to art direct. It's completely upside down. If you hire creative people, you should allow them to be creative, take what they've done and see how best to build the bridge between the given product and its potential audience. It's a sad side effect of publishers panicking about the death of the printed page. So this book was one of the most wonderfully creative challenges I've ever had, and I enjoyed every minute of my working relationship with Richard, but it was also the worst professional experience of my life.

But I don't want to end the interview on that thought... I'm hugely proud of it, and still happily take it off the shelf and re-read it.

PETE O'NEAL

Felix Lindsey "Pete" O'Neal, Jr. was born on July 27, 1940 in Kansas City, Missouri. As a young man, O'Neal had little interest in racial politics until he had a dispute with a grocer he felt wronged him. This led to O'Neal's earliest brush with racial activism when he hung up signs around the neighborhood pronouncing that the shop owner treated Black people unfairly. O'Neal's next few years were rocky ones, with a brief stint in the Navy and being arrested a handful of times for crimes ranging from stealing a radio to stabbing a man. Returning to Kansas City's 12th Street, O'Neal found work as a hustler.

Then, through a fortuitous encounter with some activist friends of his brother, O'Neal attended a protest of the United Way for their removal of support for the Black community. Through an unfortunate chain of events beginning with her spewing racial slurs in his direction, O'Neal had a run-in there with the wife of a police officer. This ultimately led to threats on his life. Amidst all of this, O'Neal traveled to Oakland, California, to request help from the newly-formed Black Panthers.

The Panthers saw his motives, as well as his fight against the police department, were wrongheaded and they declined to assist. But they saw potential in O'Neal, so they decided to keep him there and educate him. Despite his previously having little interest in social politics, O'Neal soon came to embrace the Black Panther ideology.

"The only thing I can liken this to is what I imagine that a born-again Christian experiences what they call 'the light,'" O'Neal says. "They talked to me about people like Malcolm X, who had embraced something larger than themselves for an egalitarian purpose—something that would benefit all of mankind." With tears in his eyes, O'Neal came to the realization that he could find a purpose and help others at the same time.

Following the riots of 1968 and the assassination of Martin Luther King, Jr., O'Neal began working to address the social injustices he saw in his community. O'Neal, along with Bill Whitfield, established the Kansas City chapter of the Black Panther Party. O'Neal made a point of combining forces with other African-American organizations attempting to combat racism so further progress might be made. O'Neal found that his ability to inspire others with his words, a trait that had previously come in handy hustling on the streets, now had a much more noble purpose. He had a cause to champion, and his powerful speeches brought many people into the Black Panther fold.

Under O'Neal's leadership, the Kansas City Black Panthers instituted a number of programs that were invaluable to the black community. Among them were the breakfast program for youth, a free health clinic, and free food and clothing distribution for the poor. The Black Panthers also offered anti-drug counseling.

O'Neal's Panthers soon found themselves in the spotlight

when he exposed corruption within the ranks of the Kansas City Police Department. With documents he had obtained from a retired cop, O'Neal revealed that the police were confiscating guns and then handing them over to right-wing groups like the Minutemen and the KKK. A Senate hearing investigated wrongdoing by the police department, ultimately exonerating them. In the end, O'Neal's efforts would lead to his becoming the Kansas City Police Department's public enemy number one.

Shortly thereafter, O'Neal was arrested by the SWAT Team and the FBI for "violation of the 1968 Gun Control Act." O'Neal had purchased a $19 hunting rifle from a Kansas City, Kansas pawn shop the previous year—a full year before the law had gone into effect. He was charged with carrying the gun across the state border into Missouri. O'Neal had previously been convicted as a felon in California and had his record expunged. Despite this, the attorney general planned to charge him as a convicted felon. The Gun Control Act was then amended, ensuring his conviction. At this time, he learned that the police were planning to have him murdered in prison.

Fearing for his life, O'Neal fled the country and went to Sweden. He soon relocated to Algeria, where he helped lead the international section of the Panther Party with Eldridge Cleaver. After some confusion that led many to believe O'Neal had been assassinated, he briefly disappeared in 1972, eventually turning up in Tanzania. There O'Neal and his wife Charlotte made a new life for themselves. They established a number of invaluable programs for local children. They founded the U.A.A.C.C. (the United African Alliance Community Center) in the village of Imbaseni. The center's mission statement proclaims its focus to be "healing the community by providing a diverse array of free art, music, film, and other classes to members of the community." The center also provides a hostel for travelers. Additionally, O'Neal and his wife have adopted twenty-three children whose parents could not support them.

Congressman Emmanuel Cleaver, who is O'Neal's third cousin, made many attempts to have the exiled O'Neal pardoned under Presidents Bill Clinton and Barack Obama. (O'Neal himself never asked for a pardon or participated in any way in these requests.) However, the pardon never came.

Upon learning that the 77-year-old activist was an atheist, I approached him to talk about religion and its use in the oppression of Black people in the United States, as well as his thoughts on current racial issues, Donald Trump, and the Black Lives Matter movement.

* * *

Did you grow up in a Christian household?
I did. My mother was a Catholic. I don't know if she was a practicing Catholic. My father was not as religious, but if you asked him he would have said, "Oh yes, I'm a Christian." But the key person in my life was my grandmother. We called her Mama. Now put this in all caps, she was DEVOUT. She was in church every day. She was completely committed to the Christian life and her Christian belief. If she were alive today, believe it or not, I would be hesitant to have this conversation with you. That's simply out of respect. She might just slap me in my face if she heard what I'm about to say! [Laughs.] That's the kind of environment I grew up in.

But I never was a Christian. I never believed in Santa Claus; I never believed in the Easter Bunny; and I never believed in gods. Beginning at the age of 12 I became a very pragmatic person. I don't believe in much of anything that I can't see, that I can't observe and that I can't touch. And I'd like to distinguish my atheism from agnosticism. I love astronomy, and the little bit I know about it, I know that something, some power was involved in its creation. I don't know what it was. It might have been the singularity, as they refer to the Big Bang. I don't know. But there had to be some power that created all of this complexity and all of this universal order. I accept that. But in terms of a loving, compassionate god that's aware of each and every one of us and actually cares about us —that is totally outside my area of belief. I cannot accept that.

When did you first begin to question the existence of a god?

It's so embarrassing that I'm ashamed to tell anyone, but hell, I'll tell you anyway... I was 10 years old and I wanted to go to the picture show. There was a Frankenstein movie playing, and all the kids were talking about it. The price of admission was a dime. I tried everything I could think of, but I could not get that dime. So I turned to my grandmother's god. I said, "Dear God, if you help me get this dime I'll be a good devout Christian." And of course I didn't get the dime. That started me thinking, "Is there some power that's aware of me and my desires that really cares about me?" And you know, that is just a slap in the face of all scientific thinking.

As I got older, I begin to consider this further. Right now I could go on Facebook and see some of my friends posting that God is great. "God is so great and he takes care of me." They'll get a new house and have a photograph of them holding up the key to the house. They'll say, "God is good every day. And thanks to God I've got a new house." Well, that begs the question: if God is all-caring and if he cares about the individual that got the house, then how in the hell do you explain the incredible suffering that is going on to the majority of people in the world? Is it that God is not good to them because they are poor? I simply cannot understand that type of thinking.

By that same reasoning, someone will point to God as the reason they survived a natural disaster in which hundreds of other people are killed. Does this mean that God cares more about that particular person than he did those others?

I find it ridiculous. One of my greatest heroes is Richard Dawkins. And he says something that's so profound. He said, "Without religion good people do good things and bad people do bad things. But with religion, it's the only situation where you find very good people doing very bad things." And that's what we're confronted with today. I think we have good devout human beings, but they're so blinded by their religion that they're chopping off heads, cutting and stabbing and murdering people in the name of religion. If you look at history, you'll find that some of the greatest atrocities that have ever taken place have been done in the name of religion. That is an objective fact.

I've had intelligent friends sit in my living room and tell me they believe every word of the Bible as literal truth. I say, "Literal truth? Where they're talking about stabbing and cutting off heads and stoning to death?" The Bible says that any man who denies the existence of the Holy Spirit cannot be forgiven, and that he should be stoned to death. All of this violence and all of this horrific stuff from a loving, caring God? I say no, that's absolutely not true. It can't be.

Historically Christianity has been used in the United States as a tool to control Black people and to make them subservient. Most

Black households in the United States are Christian households. There are very few Black atheists here.

And they will stick to that belief no matter what logic you put before them. That's why I don't argue about religion. How can you present facts to someone who says that their belief is based solely upon faith? There is absolutely nothing you can say. You mentioned Black folks and religion... I am completely confounded. I cannot understand why African-Americans embrace Christianity with such a fervor. This was the religion that was used to enslave them. I just cannot understand that. And they'll say, "Yes, but they weren't practicing the *real* Christianity." I say, "The real Christianity enslaves you, and it is being used to keep you subservient even today."

Do you think there is anything that can be done that will ever lessen the prevalence of Christianity within the Black community in the United States?

I have no idea and, quite frankly, I'd be afraid to try. I see people get very, very, very upset, going far beyond intellectual discussion. I respect people's rights to believe what they will, to a degree. But when that belief harms other people, how in the hell can you have respect for that?

I was married before (meeting Charlotte), many years ago. This was in the early Sixties. My father-in-law and I would go hunting. He taught me how to hunt. We would have long talks on those hunts. He was an old country man, a devout Christian. I asked him, "What if you were to die, and after your death you discovered that all of this was just a fable and had no basis in truth whatsoever?" And he told me something that has stuck with me for all of these many decades since. In his old country voice he said, "Well, I would just think it was a good way for me to live my life." Some people just really need to believe in something supernatural. Perhaps they find it difficult to come to terms with life without that belief. Just like you, I don't want to die. No one wants to die. But I can accept the fact that when I die, I'll be gone. Why would I be superior to an ant? Or a mosquito? Or a dog or cat? Why would my life have more importance than any other form of life?

Just as religion has been used to oppress Black people, it's also used as a justification to marginalize LGBT people and women.

It's absolutely horrendous. I think of abortion clinics where doctors are murdered. A while back a man in the U.S. killed a doctor. The right rallied to support him. And most of the white supremacists and neo-Nazis profess an adherence to Christian philosophy. So what is my thinking? I think it's a confused philosophy. I think it's a philosophy that has absolutely no basis in fact, and I think it's used to keep people subservient. And I'm not just talking about Black people. I think if you believe in the concept of class struggle, a great many of the working class people are Christians who believe that they're going to be rewarded in an afterlife. It's so nonsensical.

You've lived in Tanzania since 1972. Has living there changed or transformed your views regarding religion in any way?

It has. This is a very conservative country, and it's a very religious country. I am a guest in their house. I teach my children about science. Right now as we speak we're watching a documentary about astrology so they can go back and share what they've learned in school. But I never, ever, ever raise the subject of religion with them. I tell them it's entirely up to them. "You follow your heart and believe what your heart leads you to believe." That's out of respect because I am a guest in their house.

You may not know this, but back when I was in Kansas City I was charged with interrupting a religious service. There was a Methodist church in Kansas City that had a big beautiful building. When "White flight" came into being—when all of the Whites left the neighborhood because Blacks were moving in—they couldn't take the building with them. They would come back to worship in this grandiose edifice every Sunday, surrounded by extreme poverty. So we went into the church demanding that they support the uplifting of our community. They weren't receptive to the message, and a big brawl broke out. Those churches know how to fight, man! We had a big brouhaha with them. They arrested a bunch of people that day. They ended up letting everyone go except for me. They charged me with disrupting a religious service.

So back in the day I was very vocal about my non-belief. Age and time and circumstance have kind of tempered my outspokenness.

I'd like to shift gears a bit here and talk to you about some social issues. As a Black Panther yourself, what are your views on Black Lives Matter?

I think it's very on point. I don't know all of the ins and outs or the finer points in their philosophy, but anything that stands in opposition to the status quo is a good thing. I'm for it. I just think it's good that people are doing something. It's been said that if you do nothing else, then just throw a rock. Do something to stand in opposition. I like Black Lives Matter. I also liked Occupy Wall Street, although that has kind of died out. I thought that was good, but then I started hearing negative things.

You have to understand that I have been gone for 48 years. It's been nearly one half of a century. All of my views and beliefs and attitudes are secondhand. I can't base it on personal experience. I have to qualify my support and non-support in this way. I have so many people who come through here—people from every ethnic background, as well as every political and religious belief you can imagine—so I'm getting different points of view constantly. I have had to develop the ability to separate the wheat from chaff and try to discern what is true and what is not.

I think your being an American expatriate viewing all of these events from the outside gives you an ability to see things more objectively.

I cannot have etched-in-stone views. I simply cannot. I can tell you I believe it's a good thing, but it's not like back in the day when I could state these things with full certainty. And in that same sense, getting back to religion for a moment, I cannot say categorically that I am not wrong. I can tell you that with all of my senses I do not believe any of those religious myths and fables, but I cannot tell you categorically. I might die and wake up and say, "Oh, hell! They've got me in the hottest corner of hell, because I didn't know."

I'll be right there with you, Brother Pete.

This's what I'm saying! I would have a lot of good people for cellmates. We would all be sitting right there together. I remember seeing a documentary where this young fella said, "If I went to hell, I would still feel good that I stood in opposition to a mass murderer, a torturer, a racist, and an enslaver." I'm telling you the god's honest truth, it just amazes me some of the stuff I see on Facebook. And this includes my family members. They'll say, "I just found $100. God is so good." And I say, "How is God good to the guy who lost the $100?" It's mind boggling, man. But it's the world we live in. I believe there are people who find it very difficult to live in a world without an omnipotent father figure. That's really what I think it is. I think a lot of people have daddy issues, and they're trying to create a supreme daddy.

Under the Trump administration, religion is being used to inform policy more than ever before. What are your thoughts on that?

I think it's horrendous. I'm going to wax political here for a moment, but I think Trump is the epitome of capitalist avarice and evil. I've seen lots of people that I disagreed with in an extreme manner, but I could still respect their humanity. I cannot do that with this man. I think he is absolutely evil. What amazes me is that most of his followers consist of very religious people. They will hold on and support him. And here's a man who has never professed a religious thought in his life. If you look back, he never did until he ran for President. And then when he started being criticized as being ungodly, he started talking about God. I say, "Good lord, you people have lost your minds!"

You ask me what do I think? I'm going to tell you. I think America got what they deserved. I didn't like Hillary Clinton at all. But if I could have voted, I'd be damned and go to hell if I would not have voted for her. I sure the hell would have. So many people who didn't care for Hillary Clinton couldn't seem to understand that she was the lesser of two evils. People told me before the election, "Do you know there's not a nickel's worth of difference between Donald Trump and Hillary Clinton?" I said, "You're absolutely right. But if he gets into office, you're going to find out how important that four cents difference will turn out to be!" I think they are witnessing that now.

I believe Christianity laid the groundwork for Trump's election, and I'll tell you how. I think having had experience believing in and accepting a god as an absolute truth without a shred of evidence makes believing Donald Trump's outright lies a bit easier for those people to accept. His base says that facts are subjective.

I hadn't thought about that, but I think that's on the money. I think you have a very good point there. Look at what they say. They say God sent Donald Trump to make America great again. I say, "You crazy people." Understand that I am a committed socialist philosophically. I'm not a supporter of capitalism, even though I am aware that socialism has many problems that have to be overcome. But I think ultimately the world is going to have to embrace some form of socialism. I believe that with all my heart and soul. Having said that, I was not a supporter Barack Obama. But I'll tell you one thing, I think he accomplished much more than many other Presidents, particularly when you consider the economic state the United States was in when he came into office. They were talking about a depression. People seem to have forgotten that. Now they're talking about, "Look at what Trump has done for the economy." I say, "Look at the economy in 2008, and look at what it has evolved into in 2016." If there is a good economy now, as the Trumpites extoll, it didn't just magically happen when Trump got there.

As you know, Donald Trump recently remarked that African

countries are "shithole countries." What do people in Tanzania think about the United States, and have their views changed since Donald Trump took office?

I don't know what they think about the United States. The people here look at the violence and the murders, and particularly police brutality. They see this and they are amazed. They say, "Good lord, people must be crazy over there." But with Trump, even people who are not politically aware view Trump as a clown. That is the truth. If you mention Trump's name to little kids, they'll start laughing as if he was a circus clown! You mention his name and people say, "He said we live in huts and we are shitholes!" Everybody is aware of this. And I will tell you, it has diminished the way Americans are considered in general. I've seen people come here from the States and say, "I'm going to tell people I'm from Canada. I'm not going to say I'm from the States because it's embarrassing."

For a long time there were efforts being made by other people to get you a pardon from President Obama. Obviously that's not going to happen with Donald Trump. At this point, are you even interested in returning to the U.S.?

I wish I could tell you this face to face: no, I would never go back to the States. I never asked for a pardon in my life, and I never asked anyone to work on a pardon on my behalf. Never. Even when I was fighting with this wonderful lawyer who did all of this pro bono work and spent thousands of dollars of his own money to try and get my conviction overturned, I never asked him for a pardon. There was a time, however, when I felt disconnected. I thought, "I would like to see my mother." My mother is now 97 years old and she lives in a nursing home. But you know what? Technological developments changed all that. I talk to my sibling on a daily basis. I talk to my 91 year old father-in-law every night. So I no longer have that feeling of separation.

I am a very Afrocentric person. I don't know if you've ever seen the movie *Soul Food*, but one of the points is that every weekend the protagonist's family would all come together and have a big Sunday dinner together. There would always be one uncle that drinks too much and someone else who wants to start a fight. I missed those kinds of things, but technology has diminished that feeling because I can now be in contact with all of those people.

So to answer your question directly, sir, no, I do not miss the United States. I think it would be overwhelming for me now. They're moving a little too fast for me now. I have been in a laid-back African village where everything is slow and just taken in its own time. If I went back to the States, I wouldn't know what to do. I would probably stay in the house for a couple of months.

JEN PEEPLES

A lot of atheists have joked about it not taking a rocket scientist to figure out God doesn't exist. Enter Jen Peeples, an atheist spokesperson who is a real-life rocket scientist. Peeples is a true Renaissance woman; she's an aerospace engineer, a former military test pilot, and a widely respected atheist activist who co-hosts the popular television show and podcast *The Atheist Experience* as well as the acclaimed streaming show and podcast *Godless Bitches* (both affiliated with the Atheist Community of Austin).

Peeples was raised as a Christian living in the Bible Belt, but later found her way to atheism. She served in the United States Army for 26 years, where she had to hide the fact that she was gay for fear of being dishonorably discharged. She ultimately retired as a Lieutenant Colonel. Today she is able to live openly gay and she is an outspoken atheist activist.

"At this point I no longer defend atheism," she says. "I actively promote it. My life has the value, meaning, and purpose that I give it, and I'm very pleased to be affiliated with a group like the Atheist Community of Austin that shares that philosophy. Dispelling common misconceptions of atheists and promoting positive atheism as a co-host of *The Atheist Experience* is the icing on the cake."

* * *

Being someone who is both an aeronautics engineer and a fan of science fiction, I know you're very much aware of and in tune with the scientific aspect of things. Did that have anything to do with your becoming an atheist?

I was on a path to becoming an atheist from the time I was in my middle teens. I think it was probably an inevitable conclusion that I arrived at, just as a result of being institutionally indoctrinated, and just actually reading the Bible one day. And when I say one day, I one day decided I should read the Bible for myself instead of having it spoon-fed to me by various people. That was pretty much an eye-opening experience.

How long did that process take, from when you first started investigating on your own to where you realized you didn't really believe in that stuff?

There was no epiphany where I one day woke up and said, "Oh hey, I don't believe in this anymore." It was kind of a process of challenging what I thought I knew over a period of time, and gradually discarding various aspects of religion and exploring other religions' traditions. Buddhism, I looked a little bit at Shinto... Not with any intent of adopting it, but just to understand a little bit more about Eastern religions. And Wicca. I looked at all kinds of different things, one by one, working through why it is people believe things, or what they believe, and then kind of getting to the point where, in my life, subconsciously, I was applying these things to Christianity. Up until I was probably in my late twenties, I was still giving Christianity a pass on a lot of things, even though I didn't really believe in it anymore. And then after that, I started to not give Christianity a pass any longer.

You were talking about still giving it a pass in your younger twenties. Were you in the military at that time?
Yes.

A majority of the people in the military are right-wing and Christian. Do you think being in that environment contributed to some of that?
I don't know, and frankly, for most of the time I was on active duty, the Army had not been as fully penetrated by the fundamentalists as it has been now. That took a long time and didn't really reach a critical mass until the early Nineties. When I was on active duty, on my first tour in Germany, it was very clear that religion was not something you talked about at work. If you believed, that was fine, but if you didn't, then that was fine too, and you just didn't bring it to work. In fact, we had one commander when I first got to Germany who was an evangelical Christian, very fundamental with his beliefs, to the point where he didn't even think anybody should be drinking or anything like that. People talked about him behind his back and laughed at his beliefs because he was kind of a joke. That was the attitude then. It wasn't until I got off active duty and was inducted in reserves again that it became obvious that a lot of fundamentalists had penetrated the military, particularly the Army Reserve. I started butting heads with a lot of these guys. It was a little bit before that that I had stopped giving religion a pass, and some of that was what I saw people doing during

Desert Storm. Basically, using unit resources that belonged to everyone in the unit and pretending that they could be controlled exclusively by the chaplain. If you wanted access to those things, then you had to attend some kind of religious activity. That was infuriating, but then I started thinking about all the other things religion does. They claim it to be a force for good, but then they cause a lot of the problems they tend to solve.

You were an atheist lesbian in the military. Was that a tough road? What was that experience like?

That was back when you could not come out as a lesbian and expect to remain in the military. In fact, I knew people who were not gay, who were women, who were not lesbians and were investigated and ultimately discharged, because someone decided if they were a woman in the military, and they were a strong leader, they must be gay! On the one hand, you're kind of like, that's a compliment! On the other hand, it's like, wait a minute, this is being used as a weapon of sexism to eliminate women from the military. It's pretty effective. You couldn't serve openly and that has its own pitfalls.

I look back now and think of how much more effective I could've been in my years if I had been able to serve openly. For one thing, it cuts down on the rumor mill. There was, back when I was in Germany, a rumor that I was having an affair with an NCO at one of our tenements an hour away from where I was stationed. They based this on the fact that, at the time, I drove a Mustang GT Convertible. They claimed that they had seen my Mustang GT Convertible, which is a very distinctive car in Germany, outside of her apartment. There's no way because I didn't know where she lives, but the other thing is, I knew she also drove a Mustang Convertible, but it was a different color. So what they had seen was her car outside of her apartment! [Laughs.] So, you know, there's that. If only I could've served openly, I could've said, "No, I'm not seeing this NCO, and I'm actually in a relationship with another captain in another unit on this airfield." It was a much less fallacious bit of information versus fraternizing with one of my NCOs.

How did you initially get involved with The Atheist Experience?

I had been listening to the podcast. I don't remember if it was being uploaded to YouTube at the time, but I had been listening to the podcast for a while, and I knew about the Atheist Community of Austin. I guess at some point I realized, I should probably put my time and energy where my politics were and my particular beliefs were, so I really decided to seek out the ACA. I started going to the Sunday brunch. From there, I ended up at the TV studio and started hanging out there. At one point, I met Matt Dillahunty, and he was gonna talk about circumcision, but he couldn't find anybody willing to co-host with him. He knew very much about it and was willing to do something about it, and that seemed kind of controversial. It turned out I was interested in that because I'm very much opposed to routine circumcision. I feel it's a bodily rights issue. I said, "Hey, I would love to do something along these lines." So we started talking. Next thing you know, I was a guest co-host on the show with him. That show got a lot of positive feedback from fans and stuff. Next thing you know, I did another guest spot a few months later, and within a couple months I was in the regular rotation. That's kind of how it worked out.

. . .

What has that experience been like over the years? What are some of your favorite experiences on the show?

Hands down, my favorite aspect of the show is hearing from people who say we've made a positive difference in their lives. They say we either helped them shed the fear that was put there by the indoctrination, or helped them with some part of the coming out process. I think part of it is we give people a road map. Some options for how to live your life as an atheist without apology, or without hiding. That's ultimately what we want to do. Help people do that. And also, primarily, the show is about engaging with theists. We want to know what they believe, but more importantly, why they believe it. A lot of people have belief but no idea why they believe it other than, "Well, my parents told me this when I was a kid. I think it's true. They wouldn't lie to me."

The only thing I think I've regretted about doing the show is if I had known then what I know now, I probably would've used a pseudonym. On the show we use our real names, we're out there. It's kind of rare, it's not like it's an everyday thing, but there have been a few uncomfortable moments when somebody out there becomes a little too attached. You wish you had that extra layer of anonymity.

Do you ever experience the opposite side of that, running into people opposed to what you talk about or want to pick a fight?

Not in person. I'm almost never recognized around Austin, and if people do recognize me, they treat me fine. Austin's not the kind of place where if you see a celebrity, people run up and mob this person. People just pretty much go about their business. I think I've only been recognized maybe one time when I walked into a yogurt shop and the guy behind the counter brightened up. He was like, "Oh, hey, I recognize you from *The Atheist Experience!*" That was pretty much it. Otherwise, if they do, people don't say anything.

As far as people coming up and wanting to challenge me and everything, that hasn't happened in real life. I've had it happen several times on Facebook, where some random theist will send me something in my message request folder. It'll be, "Hey, I want to debate you about X, Y, Z." Depending on what they're saying, I either immediately block them or will tell them that I don't have these kind of debates on my private Facebook page, and certainly not in private. If they want that conversation, they can call they show. We can do it in public, where everyone can see it.

What are some of the weirdest calls that you can remember?
Nothing in particular stands out. There are so many people that call with so many strange ideas. They call us to talk about evolution or cosmology or something like that if they can create some kind of doubt that bolsters their belief in God. These people are just deeply confused at how it works. They just don't understand how arguments work and how reasoning and evidence work. They really don't know how to think properly about these things.

Some of the strangest calls I've gotten have been probably the anti-vaxxers who are absolutely convinced there are all these toxins. There were all these kids that were perfectly normal, then they had their MMR, and then suddenly they're all sick. I end up doing a vaccine show at least once a year, just to remind people that vaccines prevent diseases. There's no reason to be afraid of a vaccine.

Like a lot of us, you have a fascination with conspiracy theories and the people who believe them. As you know, there are some really nutso conspiracy theories out there right now, like the current "Q" conspiracy theory. It seems to me that a lot of these conspiracy theories are believed and promoted by the same people who buy into Christianity. Do you think that's true, and if so, why is that?

I don't know that there's a one-to-one correlation to religious belief and conspiracy theory belief, because I've met an awful lot of atheists who are, for example, 9/11 truthers. They need to feel like they're special in some way, and that they have some special access to what is the "truth," and that this conspiracy theory is their special knowledge about this event. I think it really does say a lot about the people who believe and promote these things. But in terms of religious belief, I don't know that there's correlation except that maybe this idea that certain religions tell people that they're special. You're saved, you're chosen by God, or something. Maybe that's the connection, that they need to be special.

The reason I say that is because the right-wing seems to come up with a lot of conspiracy theories. These days, evangelism and the right-wing seem to go hand-in-hand a lot of the time.

Like I said, I've just met an awful lot of atheists who are conspiracy theorists and stuff like that. There's atheist anti-vaxxers, there's atheists who are 9/11 truthers, and all kinds of stuff out there.

There are definitely some pretty terrible atheists out there. We're seeing a lot of sexism, a lot of gross stuff happening. Have you experienced much of that?

Yeah. There have been a lot of people who, interacting with

them online for example, decide I'm treating them badly because I disagree with whatever usual conspiracy theories they're promoting, or nonsense. There have been a few who said, "Well, I'm going to contact Matt Dillahunty about you!" Yeah, like Matt tells me what to do. Come on! There's this idea that if they perceive you're misbehaving, they'll contact the nearest male and tell him. There's a little bit of that.

As far as the sexism and right-wing misogyny in atheist circles goes, that's been going on for a long time. What's different now is that people are actually starting to be comfortable speaking up about it, saying hey, this is not okay. And of course that creates a huge backlash. When women say things about, "This is not okay," we know there's going to be huge backlash. Look at what happened to Rebecca Watson saying, "Hey guys, don't do that."

The one thing we can say about the right-wing is that they're trying their hardest to marginalize non-believers, but it seems like their efforts are having the reverse effect from what they are intending. It seems like they are inadvertently causing atheists to push back harder than ever before, becoming more and more outspoken. What are your thoughts on that?

Yeah, I think that is very much true. Part of that is, years ago, we were talking about how we were going to hit the critical number of non-believers in the population, at which point, we hit that tipping point and then things are pretty unstoppable. I think the religious right-wingers understand they are fighting a religious battle. Time isn't on their side. So I think you see a lot of desperate actions right now with trying to, for example, restrict voting access and abortion access.

Infowars is probably one of the best examples of this conspiracy theory nonsense that people consume for years.

There are other outlets out there that I think are taking a hit now as people realize, "Hey, this is not accurate and I don't subscribe to this anymore." Or maybe you have a close friend or a relative who say, "Hey, you know what? I'm not Christian anymore. I don't even believe in God." And people are feeling more able to come out. That's kind of the goal.

We were talking a little bit about this on the last episode of *Godless Bitches*. It's about community building. Part of that is empowering people just to live openly as who they are, as nonbelievers. It's one of the things that worked with the LGBTQ community. There was a need early on for the firebrands, and the riots, the rallies, the pride parades, and people getting arrested. All those things. Those had to happen to push the envelope. Part of it was, they were doing stuff that was criminalized that shouldn't have been. They got arrested for doing stuff that they should've been allowed to do anyway. And now, nobody gets arrested for that stuff. Now, gay pride is not that "we're here, we're queer, get used to it," even though we still do that. It's a celebration. We survived. All that stuff is still important, but the big thing now for atheists is just what happened with the LGBTQ community. You know what? I'm just going to live where I live, openly, without apology, and you guys have to figure out how to deal with it. And where we are as atheists too. All of us have to be willing to come out in our communities, where we can, where it's safe, and say, "Hey, I don't believe. I'm here without apology or explanation, and you guys have to figure out how to deal with that."

SETH ANDREWS

Of growing up in Tulsa, atheist activist Seth Andrews says the state of Oklahoma is known for two things: tornadoes and churches, and the tornadoes are easier to escape. Like most Oklahomans, Andrews grew up in the church, even attending Christian schools. A listener of Christian contemporary music, he eventually landed a job as a DJ hosting a morning show on a Christian radio station. Beginning with the death of a close friend in 1997, Andrews began to question his faith. Stumbling across a video of a debate between celebrated atheist Christopher Hitchens and Rabbi Shmuley Boteach in 2004, he came to the realization that he was an atheist. He stayed closeted as such until 2008, when he came out to his close family and friends. Hoping to assist other people on the verge of deconversion by sharing the things he had learned during his own transition, Andrews sought to become an atheist activist. He established a website and a Facebook page called "The Thinking Atheist."

Andrews would later begin hosting the wildly popular award-winning weekly podcast also titled *The Thinking*

Atheist, exploring virtually all aspects of religion and atheism in American society. He has said his primary mission with the podcast is to challenge unuseful stereotypes that depict atheists as being angry and religious people as stupid. Andrews also produces popular atheist-themed videos on YouTube and lectures to audiences around the world. He is the author of two books, *Deconverted: A Journey from Religion to Reason* and *Sacred Cows: A Lighthearted Look at Belief and Tradition Around the World*. Along with fellow atheist personalities Matt Dillahunty and Aron Ra, Andrews makes up one third of the activist trio affectionately known as "the Unholy Trinity."

"I'm not an enemy of religious people," Andrews has said, "but I'll be honest and say I am an enemy of religion."

* * *

You attended a Christian school as a child, and later hosted a Christian radio show for a number of years. To what do you attribute your transformation into an atheist, and ultimately an atheist activist?

My transformation came pretty late in the game, and it was a long road. I say in my book *Deconverted* that there were two major things, and about a thousand small ones. I had a few sort of cage-rattling events that made me stop and reconsider the things I had previously assumed. I came from a culture where they told us to believe first and think later. It probably had something to do with where I was in my life. I was getting a little older, and I was becoming a little less patient with people who told me to go with the flow.

I started to ask questions, going back to Genesis 1:1 and then rereading the entire Bible from the front to the back. That was a big reason. I engaged with various apologists, and the answers I got from them were not remotely satisfying. In fact, they only raised more questions. But it took a while. It was in late 2008 when I finally realized I didn't believe in any god and that I was an atheist. And because I felt like I'd been misled—not because my parents lied to me, they genuinely thought they were doing the right thing—I had been inhibited. I hadn't been properly introduced to the world. I had been raised in a culture of guilt and shame and worthlessness, a kind of slavery to bad ideas.

I hoped I could be part of the conversation. I hoped maybe I could encourage somebody else out of the faith and be a part of the solution out there. I've always been a proactive guy, so becoming an activist was a pretty easy step.

It seems like a combination of things, particularly where you live and also having had a religious background, enables you to be a more well-rounded and open-minded representative of the atheist community. It seems like you bring a different perspective, whereas a lot of atheists are very quick to mock Christians.

Well, I wasn't stupid when I was a Christian. When I first came out of the faith I saw a lot of people posting on social media who were just awful to believers. It quickly became apparent to me that they weren't really interested in helping people—they just wanted to sound superior. I genuinely want to help people. I think religion enslaves, so let's try to go out and see these people for who they are. Matt Dillahunty was going to be a Baptist minister at one point, but he wasn't an idiot. He was a victim of bad ideas, of indoctrination, and cultural reinforcement.

Some of the best people I know believe in god. I'm married to someone who believes in god, and she's the most beautiful person I know. So this whole idea that they're some sort of second-class citizen is just wrong. We come to different conclusions on the god question, and I think many of [those conclusions] are just products of family and culture, but they don't deserve this awful treatment that they receive out there. And if I was coming out of the faith, or if someone had challenged me and wanted me to defend my faith, are they really going to insult me into a better idea? You're not going to browbeat someone into an epiphany. You can't kick them in the teeth and tell them they're stupid and then expect them to listen to anything you have to say. They'll double down because they're in defense mode. They're not going to listen. I want to have a conversation. Let's talk. People are people. You'll find amazing Christians and horrible, awful Christians. You'll find amazing, wonderful atheists, and you'll find just the worst atheists in the world. [Laughs.] People are people in every culture.

With your wife being a Christian, how does that work at home? Obviously you try to be open-minded towards one another, but do problems ever arise from that?

We've had our moments. It helps that she's not a fundamentalist. She's a borderline deist. She was raised Christian, but she doesn't attend church or read the Bible. She doesn't pray before meals. She's Christian in the most casual sense. You know, "I think there's something out there." She's really more a deist, but Christianity is where she's the most comfortable. It gives her comfort and she enjoys it.

We've had our moments. Sometimes we look each other in the eye and it's like we're different nations. We're not speaking the same language, we don't get each other. It's like, "Come on, I wish you'd see my point of view!" Those moments are frustrating. It's difficult to share a life with someone who disagrees on a critical question. Beyond that, what I appreciate about Natalie is that, unlike my mother and father, she supports my right to be me. It's about mutual respect. Natalie's life is hers to live. She looks at me and she's like, "You and me have some disagreements, but you need to be you, whoever that is. I totally support you in what you are about. So go be who you need to be." She travels with me, and occasionally she'll come out and work the book table with me. She supports me when I'm working on various productions. She likes to hear about my work and what I'm doing. It's all about supporting my right to live my own life on my terms, and that's how we've made it work. It's sometimes amazingly difficult, but aside from those occasional speed bumps, the rest of it is good enough to have made it all worth it.

I'm dating for the first time in many years, and I had no idea how difficult it was going to be dating as an atheist in the Midwest. For a lot of people, atheism is a deal-breaker.

At least it's good to know that upfront. What breaks my heart is when you have two people who believed devoutly. Maybe they have two or three children. And then fifteen years into the relationship, one of the couple comes to the point of non-belief and says, "I just don't buy this." Then the spouse feels like they've had the carpet pulled out from underneath them. "Hey, wait a minute, I thought we were going to raise our kids in the Christian church. I thought I would have a life partner who would share my faith. That's the deal I made." Before you know it, they've gone through the gauntlet of relationship problems and counseling and divorce and custody of the kids. Those things can be tremendously awful, so the one good thing is that if you're on the front end, you can sort of frontload the criteria and find someone who shares your value system to a degree and there are no surprises.

. . .

You've stated in the past that Christopher Hitchens' work had an impact on you early on. Would you care to talk a little bit about that?

I had seen him do some television interviews from time to time, and I just Google searched him once because he just had a real style about him, you know? I ended up watching this debate between himself and this rabbi, Rabbi Shmuley Boteach, and Hitchens just really blew me away. I thought, "This guy isn't a malcontent, he's not frothing at the mouth and pounding at the podium. He seems to have good humor and compassion for people. He's interested in what's true and he doesn't put up with any crap." I thought that was terrific.

Once I had seen that exchange, I then found myself seeking out all kinds of Christopher Hitchens' stuff. That avalanched into a bunch of other names I hadn't heard of. Who's this Richard Dawkins guy? Who's Charles Templeton? Who's Dan Barker? Then I had to buy their books... I was obsessed. I was reading and watching and sponging up information to a degree that people around me thought I had lost it. But I was just making up for lost time. Why had I never heard about these people? Why had I never been introduced to this information? Where had they been? Of course that was the wrong question. The real question was, where had I been? I had been in a cocoon of indoctrination and cultural reinforcement. Once I busted out, that was a liberating moment.

You interviewed Richard Dawkins. Tell me about that experience.

He's never been anything but really cordial to me. I've actually interviewed him on three different occasions. I can't overstate how instrumental his book *The God Delusion* was for me. I know it's become cliché to say that, but that book is a game-changer. It changed my life. I told him so the first time I met him at the 2012 Reason Rally. I was like, "Your book changed my life. It changed everything for me." In the times I've had the chance to be around him, he's very proper and very British. It's not like walking out and seeing Penn Jillette or Aron Ra or Matt Dillahunty, where you say, "How are you? Let's go out and get a beer!" Dawkins is always very much in his own head, but he's always been pleasant and extremely kind. And he's just pawed at everywhere he goes, so the fact that he would give me the time of day and the time to have these conversations was a real honor. I still to this day appreciate his work, because it was there for me at a critical time. I believe *The God Delusion* is one of the most well-articulated arguments against the defenses of God out there. It's fantastic.

You mentioned your pals Aron Ra and Matt Dillahunty. I wondered if you might like to talk about their work and also what it's like to work with them?

I met them when I first came out as an atheist. You have to understand, I was a Christian radio host for 12 years and I segued into pop and rock radio until 2004, when I became a video producer. Eighty percent of the clientele of the company I worked for was churches. I was really good at it. I helped to raise a lot of money for churches, so now I get to do my penance for all that. [Laughs.] I was still working for this company. My employers were Christian and my whole family was Christian. I was coming out of an 18-year marriage at that time. So when I first realized I was an atheist, I wanted desperately to be part of the conversation but I wasn't ready to show my face yet because, man, what if they fire me? I had a mortgage to pay and responsibilities. What would happen?

So *The Thinking Atheist*'s icon was all people knew about

me. They knew my first name when the radio podcast went live in 2010, but nobody saw my face until the summer of 2011. I was finally at that point where I said, "Let's just pull the trigger on this. It's time to own it." So I took the stage at FreeOK, the Oklahoma Free Thought Conference, which was held at All Souls Unitarian Church in Tulsa. I took the stage and I was like, "Hello, world!" On the roster that day were Matt Dillahunty and Aron Ra. I had never met them in person before, and we all just instantly clicked. We just became buddies. Over the course of time that friendship strengthened. I called them in 2012 and said, "What if we all did this speaking tour together? Just for the hell of it. What if we called it the Unholy Trinity?" And they thought that was big fun, so we did that in the Spring of 2013. Then we were invited to speak in Australia in the Spring of 2014, and we did three cities there. We retired the tour after that because we were starting to get pigeonholed, but they remain my brothers to this day.

They are two of my favorite people in the world. They have a tremendous heart for people. They have a tremendous desire to see superstitious ideas defeated and to see an evidence-based world. I have a real admiration and respect for those guys.

As you know, we live in an era where a lot of Americans don't trust facts that are genuinely provable. Do you think this mindset is a byproduct of Christianity, and do you see much hope for the future in regards to this dismissal of truth?

It's an interesting phenomenon, because you'll find that non-religious people don't trust facts. I know one person in particular who's an atheist who is a flat-earth guy. I just don't know how this happens. You'll find people who are atheists who are atheists for irrational reasons. You know, "aliens told me there is no God." That's an atheist, but he's not a rationalist.

You'll find people who are just flawed human beings who are capable of holding some pretty awful ideas in all walks of life.

I think religion certainly does feed that beast. It's probably one of the driving forces behind this suspicion of facts. I was raised in a culture where we were told to be hugely suspicious of scientists. "Don't trust science. Read the Bible." If science happens to line up with what the Bible says, then now it's verification. A-ha! Science lines up, so that means it's true! And then all the other science that spoke about things like evolution and the Big Bang, well, that's all a lie of Satan and part of the Star Chamber Conspiracy of scientists who want to kill God. So I think a lot of it is religion-born, but human beings are all guilty of rooting for what we want to be true. We're all guilty of confirmation bias. We're all guilty of seeing a headline or social media post in line with what we already think, and we forward or share it before we've even finished the article. We in the atheist culture need to be better skeptics, because we're guilty of spreading bad info just like everyone else. Who wrote it? Where did it come from? What does the science say? Who checked them? All of these questions need to come into play.

And then you've got someone like Donald Trump, who is selling the narrative that you can't trust the media. He starts poking at that fire, and that doesn't help us at all either. It's kind of a frightening time. The upside is that the nature of the Internet—the fact that it is such a Wild Wild West out there, and many people know it—is training some people to do a better job of being suspicious. You're seeing people saying, "Did you see it on the Internet?" Their first inclination is to be skeptical. There is some of that going on, and I find that encouraging.

I personally feel that everyone has something to fear with the

Trump administration. But do you feel that atheists in particular have something to fear? Are there things that are specific to the atheist community that we should be afraid of in regards to this administration?

Politics is tough. I always get myself into trouble here, because there is a group of pro-Trump atheists. When you talk politics they say, "You talk like all atheists are liberals, and we're not." But from my perspective, I think so much of what is said and done out there in the political narratives are rooted in or excused by religion. You've got Donald Trump saying, "We're going to put Merry Christmas back in the holiday again!" He says that like no one was able to say 'Merry Christmas'. [Laughs.] That's just totally bogus. That's a sort of persecution narrative that's sold by Christianity. You've got his wife reading the Lord's Prayer at public events, and you've got all these evangelical Christian politicians saying he's God's appointment...

Beyond that you see the fights where some theocrats are trying to tell us what marriage is, that it's a union between a man and a woman. They're trying to tell us what healthy sexuality is. Not what science says it is, but what religion says it is. They're trying to determine who gets what rights and those are quite often religious conversations. What's taught to our children in science textbooks... These are things that are affected by religion. In almost every instance, from my perspective, those who are trying to break down the separation of church and state are people who align with the Republican party. I'm not saying all Republican party members are religious, but they lean heavily in that direction. Those messages play loudly and often. It is the progressive, it is the liberal, it is the person on the left who is out there fighting against discrimination against gays and fighting for the rights of women. They're fighting for true science to be taught in our science books.

So I think our non-belief in deities can speak to what we

think and what we promote and how we vote. Those things do come into play.

What factors led you to back out of appearing at MythCon 2017, and do you stand by that decision today?

For those who aren't aware of what MythCon is, it's an event that's been going on in Milwaukee for a few years. Atheists have a lot of different conventions. This one was sponsored and organized by Mythicist Milwaukee. At the beginning of the year they asked me if I wanted to come and be a guest at a movie premiere for a film that they produced called *Batman & Jesus*. They weren't asking me to speak, they just asked me if I wanted to come. I do 35 speaking dates a year. I singlehandedly produce a radio podcast every week. I'm producing videos. I'm busy, very active in my own community. I don't follow too much on what's happening at any individual conference until I get pretty close to it and start promoting it. But I saw the MythCon guys at American Atheist. They took me aside and said, "Have you heard about all this big controversy" I said no, I hadn't. They said they had invited a controversial YouTuber named Sargon of Akkad who had said some pretty nasty and horrible stuff. They were framing it as an invitation to dialogue. "Let's bring in these separate sides and make this about discourse." I was like, "Okay, fine."

Then after that things got really nasty. There was a group of people who had some really serious concerns that this Sargon of Akkad guy was horrible towards women. He aligned feminism with autism. He told someone publicly in a tweet, as a taunt, "I wouldn't even rape you." There was some much-justifiable criticism for having him on the roster. Then beyond that, you had some people who just lost their minds and said that anybody who would ever attend or support

MythCon was an enabler of Sargon's alt-right white supremacist stuff—whatever they were saying he was. "You are complicit. You're anti-human rights. You're anti-feminist. You're anti-equality." Then you had MythCon over here saying, "It's just a free speech exercise. We think the conference models out there are waning, and it's time to shake things up. We think this is the conference model for the 21st century."

More and more people were dropping out. There was a circus atmosphere around the whole thing. I defend Myth-Con's right to invite whomever they want. They shouldn't have to deal with threats. They shouldn't have to deal with people calling the hotel and telling them there's going to be dangerous people there who might potentially accost or assault people. The speakers and attendees have every right to go without being threatened or labeled as Nazis or rape apologists.

When I got further and further into this with the MythCon guys, I became increasingly convinced that they are monumentally-naive or just have damaged ideas about what the atheist movement is, what it means, and who should be represented on stage. I think they were naïve and reckless. None of this is why I do conferences. I didn't sign up for this. I go to communicate ideas, to learn new things, and to foster community. It's not that I don't want to be challenged. I do want to be challenged. And you do see that at our conferences, but you don't have to bring out bottom-feeders and allow them time in the sun on our dime in order to legitimize themselves.

It was a lose-lose situation for me. If I had gone up and spoken, then I'd be a loser and a horrible person and a Nazi sympathizer. I finally decided that the white noise of the event was not even remotely worth it. I called them and said, "I'm out. This is just a circus. This is crazy. I don't want to do this." So now I'm a coward, or even worse, I pulled out too late and didn't have the spine to make a stand in the beginning. Everyone dragged their own soapbox in.

The death of discourse is one thing that again this event has revealed. What alarms me isn't legitimate criticism and passionate disagreement, which I think we need, but the character assassination and vilification. You've got people calling each other garbage humans because they disagree with each other on a point at MythCon. They had people calling each other Nazis and trying to destroy one another left and right. What happened to us being able to see each other for who we are? Many of the names in question beyond myself, like Matt Dillahunty. I know the guy. He loves people. He wants the best ideas to win. He cares about equality. He's certainly not a white supremacist, but those were allegations thrown in his direction.

At the end of the day, it's been a few weeks now, and people are still chewing each other up over this. It just hurts the heart. It's not that we don't call out horrible people doing horrible things, and Sargon of Akkad certainly qualifies, but that whole circus ends up helping him more than anyone else. We're not going to get discourse. He's just going to get some time in the sun. He and his band of merry malcontents are going to show up and cheer about the rape tweet.

It's interesting in the aftermath to watch some people who are using MythCon to declare the death of the entire atheist movement. It's crazy. It's absolutely insane. We have gatherings; we have events; we have community; we have organizations who are fighting the fight and doing important work; we have wonderful activists at every tier, who are engaged in making a difference. I'm doing a show on my own broadcast asking the question, "Is the atheist movement dying?" And I'll give you the answer, and the answer is "no." Of course it's not dying. We have some problems. We have bigots in our midst, we do. But Matt Dillahunty's not one of them. There are some people who have horrible ideas out there under the atheism banner, and we have to address that, but we're not going to address it by tearing each other to shreds publicly.

I can only grieve when I think there might be a religious person who was where I once was when I was coming out of the faith, asking themselves, "What is an atheist?" If I had been in that situation and I had Googled that and had stumbled upon this name-calling and all of this horrible behavior, I probably would have run in the other direction. I wouldn't have wanted anything to do with these people. Is this what we're offering people? That they can come out of superstition so they can declare other enemies and spend all of your time telling them that they're horrible garbage humans? I have optimism that we'll get past all of this, but I have no plans to participate with anything MythCon does moving forward unless something dramatically changes.

KEITH LOWELL JENSEN

Comic Keith Lowell Jensen began working in comedy at the age of ten, performing ventriloquism and reenacting Abbott and Costello routines. As a teen, Jensen dropped out of high school and joined *Spike and Mike's Festival of Animation*, touring throughout the United States and Canada.

In 2009, Jensen released his first comedy album, *To the Moon*. Two years later he followed this up with *Cats Made of Rabbits*. His third album was *Elf Orgy* in 2013, and then the popular *Atheist Christmas*, complete with accompanying standup DVD.

Labeled as an atheist comedian, there is more to Keith Lowell Jensen than just his disbelief. This comedian and activist is the straight host of *The Gay and Lesbian Comedy Show*. He is the non-disabled founder and sometimes host of *The Comedians with Disabilities Act*. He is a non-pot smoker who frequently performs at pot legalization benefits. He also serves as the atheist representative on *The Coexist Comedy Tour*, which features comic representatives from a variety of religions. He has toured with the likes of Norm MacDonald, Robin Williams, and Doug Stanhope.

His opinions and musings can be found on his blog page at RockAss.net.

* * *

Have you always been an atheist? What is your background in regards to religion?

I grew up Catholic. I was baptized, and I made first communion. I was a pretty troubled kid, so after getting expelled for the second time, my mom let some neighbors take me to a small, apostolic church. I really got into it. It was sort of a born again, charismatic type thing. My mom and my brothers with her, we all sort of converted together out of Catholicism. That lasted a couple of years, and then I started losing my faith when I was fourteen or fifteen.

When did it occur to you to mix your atheism with comedy?

I talk about all aspects of my life and my experiences in my comedy, but the atheism didn't really come up that much until after September 11th, which was the first time I really felt at odds with religion. I mean, I feel like in a lot of ways that little apostolic church we went to did me a lot of good; not the religious aspect of it, but the community aspect of it. There were some wonderful people there, and I still have some very warm feelings towards those people. I don't think I'm quite as reactive as a lot of atheists that started out religious. So after September 11th I started seeing us really hit by fundamentalists and then seeing America want to respond by becoming more fundamentalist. That kind of woke up the more outspoken atheist in me, I guess.

And the first routine I did addressing my atheism, which you can still find on YouTube under "atheist comedian," addressed that specifically. It addressed an e-mail I had gotten in regards to 9/11 and the thoughts it triggered in me. I think that material really resonated with people. That video on YouTube took off more than anything else I've ever posted. And then I started getting approached by atheist conventions and atheist groups from around the country and asked to come and perform.

It was at that time that myself and a friend of mine, who is Hindu and was actually on that same show as me, started something called the *Coexist Comedy Tour*. I never really planned to brand myself the "atheist comedian," and I still don't really, but on the *Coexist Comedy Tour* I was the atheist. He was the Hindu, someone else was the Muslim, someone else was the Buddhist. With the rest of them that didn't really stick. They were only that title on that tour. With me, it stuck more. People were like, "Yeah, that's the atheist comedian." I do plenty of shows where I'll go the whole hour and barely mention my atheism, but I don't really resist it either. I'm like, "That's fine. I'm the atheist comedian. I don't give a shit." [Laughs.]

I've heard that a lot of comedians are actually atheists. Is that true?

Yeah. A lot of comedians tease me about that. They're like, "You're the atheist comedian, are you? Why not the male comedian?" Not really a distinction, but really it's just a matter of how much you choose to address it. And truthfully, a lot of comics choose to address it, as well. So I guess what sets me apart is being willing to be an atheist activist, and be active within the atheist community in sort of organized atheism. It's funny, I don't know how much I would be a part of that if it weren't for finding a place for myself in that community as a comedian. My wife tried to take me to an atheist meet-up group one time out of her thinking I would be interested in it, and they listed the address wrong. We ended up at a baptism! [Laughs.] I walked in and said, "I don't think this is it, honey." But it wasn't something I had sought out that much—taking an active role in it. But I really enjoy that now. I like being a part of it.

What's the difference between performing somewhere like Skepticon as opposed to a comedy club?
There's a lot that's the same. You know, I have the same job to do. I think it's funny that at Skepticon it's much more likely that people are going to be live tweeting my performance. That always cracks me up to come off stage and see that some quote of something I said is being re-tweeted.

There is sort of this "Inside Baseball" stuff… There are ways I can make fun of the atheist community when I'm at a meeting like that, where the references might go over people's heads in a club. I can make it more specific. You know, if I'm joking about it in the club, I'm maybe joking more about the concept of atheism or just getting along with the rest of the world as an atheist. When I'm talking about it at Skepticon, I actually talk about the community itself and some of the experiences that we have as a community.

When you perform regular shows, do you get many walk-outs from the non-secular crowd?
No. I feel like my style is very non-abrasive, both by natural instinct and by design. I'm not super reactive. I try not to have a chip on my shoulder. My oldest brother, whom I love dearly, is

a Christian minister. My Mom is Christian. I have a lot of dear friends who are Muslim, so I try to come across very friendly. I even talk in my latest special, which isn't out yet, about the Jehovah Witnesses coming to the door. My wife's response to them is, "We're an atheist family." She says it with a big smile on her face. I like that. I feel like that's how it should be said. Often those of us who grew up religious...we don't say it like that. We say it with an expectation of outrage from the person we're saying it to. We say it with a chip on our shoulder. But why not say it like that? "We're atheists. Across the street are Muslims. The people two doors down are Hindu. We all think you're wrong, but we get together and have barbecues and you're totally welcome to come." [Laughs.]

I try to be friendly like that. I also apply something called the Dick Gregory Rule, after the great civil rights comedian, Dick Gregory. They asked him about making fun of race and white people in particular to a white audience during such a difficult time and how he managed to get away with it. He said the rule he followed was that he always made fun of himself first. Once he made fun of himself, he was pretty free to make fun of them. So I do have bits that make fun of myself. I have a bit on one of my albums about being at a Rapture Day party when an earthquake hits, and being in a room full of atheists on Rapture Day. It's really fun. [Laughs again.] And I make fun of us being organized, as well, and the difficulties inherent in that. People laugh with me. And if they're willing to laugh at me, then I'm willing to laugh at myself, and then most of them are good sports when I flip it. That includes performing at places like Nevada, where a guy came up to me afterward and said, "Are you really an atheist?" I said, "Yeah. It would kind of be weird if I wasn't." [Chuckles.] He said, "Can I get a picture with you?" He said, "I've never met an atheist before." I was like, "Oh, I think you have." But I posed for the picture and I thought it was great. I was like an atheism ambassador of sorts.

Have you had many people attempt to convert you in your lifetime?

Oh, sure! I mean, me and my oldest brother, the minister, we had a real hard go of it in the early years of my adulthood. Then we finally reached a point where we agreed just not to talk about religion anymore. Part of it was that, for him, it was talking about something from an attached, very emotional place. For me, it was just intellectualizing. So now we just concentrate on the things we have in common. We're both extremely liberal. Our sense of morality is very, very similar. We talk about that. I mean, people want to try to convert you constantly.

You're also a parent. Sometimes as an atheist parent it's difficult to know how to best proceed with your children in terms of religion. What's been your approach to that?

It was so funny... We were driving, and my daughter was about five at the time, and she said, "Daddy, I'm not an atheist." I said, "Okay, sweetie." She said, "I believe in all the gods and all the goddesses." I said, "Yeah?" And she said, "Yeah. I don't worship them or honor them," which are terms I think she picked up from the Greek myths that she learned about. She said, "But I believe in them." Then she continued with her list. "And also fairies. And mermaids." I was like, "Right on." [Laughs.] I mean, what are you gonna do if your daughter's not an atheist? That's just not something that crosses my mind. I want my daughter to know how to think critically, and how to apply logic. I want her to draw the conclusions she draws on her own. Hopefully those will evolve and change all throughout her life. That's much more important to me than for her to reach any specific conclusions.

There is the obligation to point out that we're the odd ones out in the family. "Grandma goes to church every Sunday. We'll go to church with Grandma on Easter"—although I've only been in town like once in the last eight Easters. [Laughs.] I do a pretty good job of being booked then. I was in China this last Easter, so I really went a long way to avoid it. They didn't do much of an Easter in China. That's an interesting discussion. It's like, "You know the Greek myths? Well, Grandma has a myth she believes in that's similar. She doesn't think it's a myth, but I do." I just try to be really open and honest about it and let her draw her own conclusions.

What was the idea behind Atheist Christmas?

One thing that a lot of people just didn't get is that it's fun. There's more to it beyond that, but I just think it's a fun title. I love Christmas. I grew up celebrating Christmas. It's part of my cultural tradition and family tradition, but I'm not going to stop just because I don't believe Jesus was magic anymore than I'm going to when I stopped believing Santa Claus was real. [Laughs.] It's still all fun. It was just a joke on that, the whole "war on Christmas" thing. I'm saying, "There's no war here. I love it." You guys are willing to share it with me, right? You guys are willing to let me celebrate your holiday? I think we should have more reasons to celebrate, not less. I'm down. No one questions what you believe when you celebrate Halloween or St. Patrick's Day. Those are just fun holidays. There are little traditions that go with them that are just fun—most of them very specifically American. They have nothing to do with where these holidays even came from.

. . .

I read that in December a religious woman confronted you about "The Banana Story."

I don't know if it was a religious woman necessarily, but she was definitely more conservative. That story is a fairly nuanced story about giving the sex talk to a young man who, as far as we knew, was now sexually active. We performed it in an art gallery, of all places. This was a fairly liberal, sophisticated audience. And she comes up to me afterwards and says, "Oh, that was pretty rough." I said, "What do you mean rough?" When comedians say rough, we mean unpolished. She said, "You were talking about a little boy and banana with a condom on it." I said, "Whoa! That actually sounds very different from what I was talking about!" There was a very important context to those things. She said, "Why would you talk to a young person about those things?" And I said, "Because you have to. If you don't, they go and get STDs or get pregnant." Then she basically gave me an abstinence-only education response to it. She said, "Well, I think you just shouldn't talk to them about it." I said, "Well, there were a lot of states that volunteered to do that experiment for us, and what they got was soaring teen pregnancy rates and STD outbreaks. So, no." I looked at her and said, "Listen, it sounds like you didn't so much take issue with me as a comedian, but rather you just disagree with my beliefs. And that's fine. You're entitled to that." I said, "You're in an art gallery. Look at all these paintings around you... You may not like or agree with all of them, and the people who painted them are not obligated in any way to give a shit what you think." And I turned and walked away from her. [Laughs again.] And that was that.

But then we had a second show, and I did the banana joke again, and then followed it up by telling them what had just happened. That brought the house down. That was great that she gifted me that. It was very funny because we had an early show and a late show. The early show was very stiff and older... people that thought they could buy their way into being intellectuals and members of that museum. [Laughs.] They were just awful. And then we had our late show, and everyone had had some wine and was cool and relaxed. It was a younger crowd. It was so much more fun. Just a difference between night and day.

CASEYRENEE LOPEZ

Caseyrenee Lopez is a queer, atheist poet hailing from the Deep South, a place where being queer and atheist isn't commonly accepted. This hasn't slowed Lopez down much. Lopez is the editor of *Crab Fat Magazine*, which publishes fiction nonfiction, and poetry. In addition, Lopez founded and operates Damaged Goods Press, which publishes experimental work by queer and trans artists.

Lopez published their first collection of original poetry in 2016 with the chapbook *QueerSexWords*. Since then, they have produced the full-length collections *the new gods* and *i was born dead*, both published in 2018. Lopez has yet another collection, a chapbook titled *heretic bastard*, coming soon.

Lopez has worked as an editor at *Stirring*, *TQ Review: A Journal of Trans & Queer Voices*, *Twisted Vine Literary Arts Journal*, and *Mistress Magazine*. In addition to their work as a poet, Lopez also works as an adjunct English professor at both Georgia Military College and John Tyler Community College.

* * *

You identify using the we/they pronouns. For the uninitiated, what exactly does that signify?

For me personally, it's about removing unnecessary gender in the way we see people and talk to people. For other people, it has a lot to do with not fitting one definition or the other, I think.

What type of environment did you grow up in, in terms of religion?

Really no kind of religion. My parents, they said they believed in God, but it was never anything that was organized or really talked about in our house. Even as a kid, I never had a church or went to church. If I did, it was because I had friends who went and asked me to go with them. It was never anything important to me, and I was never made to feel different because of it.

When did you realize you were an atheist?

I think I started knowing when I was a teenager, probably 15 or 16 years old. This was maybe 10th, 11th grade in high school. But at that time, I also was practicing witchcraft and Wicca. I don't really know if there was a catalyst that turned me off from spirituality, religion, or any sort of deified worship. It just never made sense to me. Nobody could ever explain it. Even people working within the church, theologians, philosophers, or friends in academia. Nobody can explain it to me in a way that makes sense enough that I should put all my eggs in one basket. From day one, once I realized that I could think for myself and be my own person, I never had any belief.

As I've gotten older, I have increasingly become a lot more vocal about my atheism; some people would even say militant, but I disagree with that. I definitely don't push my beliefs off on other people. I'm very much a "keep your beliefs to yourself" kind of person. It took awhile for me to finally just say I was absolutely an atheist. But now I'm a convinced atheist. I'm not agnostic, I'm not skeptical, I just do not believe.

You mentioned some people say you're militant. Why do you think that is?

You know, I think that perception just kind of comes with it. It plays into the rhetoric that atheists are negative, bad, immoral people. When you hear somebody say 'militant Christian,' you think one of two things: they're either extreme in their beliefs and value system, or they push it on other people. It's like, by the way of the sword I'm going to kill you. You know how it goes. And that applies to atheism as well. You say 'militant atheist,' then, well, you're just going to bully people into seeing things the way you see it. I really don't see it that way at all. It's more a case of standing your ground and upholding your own beliefs, or lack thereof, instead of essentially letting this Christian world we're built around bully us into submission.

There's that stereotype that atheists are militant and want to push an agenda on others. It seems ironic that the people who believe that are the ones pushing their Christian agenda on everyone else.

I think that you're right. I think that people like to say a lot of words but never really know what they're after, or the point they're trying to make. It's just, "Let me say what I think would be buzzwords to catch people's attention." Then it really comes down to, do you really know what you're talking about? It basically boils down to if the shoe fits. These people who make these claims, they're obviously just these sweeping generalizations of all different kinds of people. It comes down to, are you saying it because you see it in yourself? Why are you actually saying this? As far as I know, I have never, ever, in the media, or any sort of actual fair, neutral media, seen atheists being horrible people. Last time I checked, it's the religious who murder and rape and essentially oppress other people.

The religious right's guy, Donald Trump, does that. Anything he does, he then accuses other people of doing. It's kind of that same thing.

I definitely don't think that you're wrong. On that kind of level, Trump is just a mouthpiece for the religious right. That's it. They will look any way, except head on, at what he's saying or doing. They're going to look in any other direction, point fingers at any other kind of people, because if it doesn't align with their beliefs, whether it's coming from a charlatan or not, then you're the enemy.

At what ages did you come out to your family that you were queer and an atheist? And how were things met?

I officially came out as queer when I was 17. Nothing actually happened. My mom kind of shrugged, laughed in my face a little bit, and said, "Oh, okay. I've known since you were 12, but I guess it's cool you're telling me now." So that was just kind of like, wow. To this day, it's not a big deal. She literally could not care less about that part of my life. She just wants me to be happy and live in a way that she was never able to live; to live a better life.

As far as my religion, or lack thereof…my atheism… My family doesn't care. It's never been an issue because we're all kind of an eclectic bunch. When I was really little, my grandma was really into the occult. She read tarot and read people's palms. She was kind of known in our local community as the one who was "in touch" and people would come and see her, but she also identified as a Christian. We had a family Bible. She never went to church, I never saw her pray or anything. That was kind of the attitude throughout my whole life and in my whole family. You can believe in God or not, it's your actions that determine what kind of person you are.

People who read this interview may not initially understand why we're talking about sexual orientation in a book about atheism. But I think religion is the primary obstacle for the LBGT community achieving social equality in this society and in the world. What are your thoughts on that?

I personally don't have a lot of thoughts about that specifically because of the way I was brought up. Religion has never really been an influencing factor in my life. I will say I have had friends who have struggled really, really bad, like self-loathing, suicidal thoughts, severe onset depression, because their religion and religious community did not accept that they were gay, queer, lesbian, bi, or trans. I've seen it from an outside perspective, but personally, I haven't been influenced in that sort of intimate way. I can say though, with the religious right getting its way into politics and moving away from the wall of separation of church and state... We move forward, but we then step back every couple of years. They are always chipping away at women's rights, reproductive rights, queer rights. It's only been three years that I've been legally allowed to marry my husband and we've been together for the better part of 13 years. That's the kind of impact I see. It's on a macro-scale, I guess.

* * *

Do you have hope that things will get better in this country any time soon?

I do. I think it's happening now. People get scared when things change and what they think of as being "too fast." But people don't want to go back in time either. It's always going to be, we take a step forward, and then people freak out and get scared so we might stumble, or find this muddled area where we get caught up. Ultimately, we're going to keep going forward. There's no going back from here. This has been something since the founding of America. We've always had these progressive ideas, but putting them into practice has been the problem. Over the past 10 years, there has been a major influx of people saying, "I'm not religious. I don't care for this. I don't like the way that these conservative ideals are holding us back." People my age and younger are getting out to vote. We're getting rid of these institutions. And I think that's something that happens with almost every generation. It's just the issues maybe look different, times are different now. We have so much more connection to social media and what have you. But ultimately, yeah, we're going to make the change and it's going to stick. Right now, it's just one of those muddled, scared, confused kind of places, but it's nothing that's going to be permanent.

In what ways do your sexuality and atheism inform your writing?

Those things are absolutely foundational to my writing. I would not be writing anything without essentially embracing those parts of myself. I lean in heavily to themes that stem from being queer in this country and growing up in the deep south of

Georgia, where it's not only pretty queer-phobic there, but so entrenched in those conservative, religious beliefs. My writing is a means of putting myself out there and saying, "Hey guys, queer people and atheist people do exist in the deep south of Georgia. We may be a little bit marooned on an island, but we're here! Please don't erase us or forget that we're here! We're not all conservative, confederacy-loving folks."

You talked a little bit about trying not to be loud and pushy about religion. Do you feel like your poetry gives you an outlet where it's safer and more acceptable to voice those things?

Yeah! I definitely do. Especially when you look at the landscape of the way poetry in general, or writing in general is headed. On the mainstream, it's a much more progressive, accepting field as it were, than for me to get up on a soap box and deliver a sermon about different facets of my identity, or different facets of being an atheist. People respond to it a lot better when it can be put in a way that is perhaps more relatable or understandable, and it's not just thrown to them.

I feel like people who buy your books are going to have an idea of who you are and what your writing entails, so you're going to get less of those extreme, right-winged people.

Oh, absolutely. I would like to reach folks on the other side of the aisle, but I don't think we're quite there yet.

GEORGE PERDIKIS

Mooloolaba, Queensland (Australia) schoolmates George Perdikis and Peter Furler established a rock band known as The News in 1985. Perdikis (guitarist), Furler (drummer), John James (lead singer), and Sean Taylor (bass) then transformed the band into a Christian rock band. "Peter and I started jamming back in 1981," Perdikis recalls. "We jammed for a few years at my place, just doing covers and mucking around. It wasn't until 1985, when Peter's family had moved to a different state that we officially founded the band." Perdikis was in the Air Force at the time, and eventually left to follow his dreams of being a professional musician. In 1987, they inked a deal with Refuge Communications. They retitled the band The Newsboys to avoid conflict with Huey Lewis and the News, and the rest is history.

The Newsboys landed on American shores on Christmas Day, 1987. The band recorded their first album, *Read All About It*, in about a week. Soon they were playing big venues like Creation Fest and Atlanta Fest, and they took the scene by storm, ultimately becoming one of the biggest Christian pop bands of all time.

In 1990, Perdikis left the band after they recorded their second album, *Hell Is for Wimps*. In January 2015, Perdikis showed that there was more than one way for a Christian rock star to make headlines when he announced that he was now an atheist.

We all know that many Christians believe rock music is the devil's music. When you were playing rock music for God, did people still tell you you were going to hell for playing it?

Oh, yeah. Before we got signed we were involved with a church in Nambour on the Sunshine Coast, Queensland. It was a big church. One time we did a gig at a pub playing half covers and half original songs and the pastor of the church found out that many of the youth had come to see us play. All of a sudden, we were doing the music of the devil! We got a lot of flak from the church, but we didn't care. We were rebellious youth. We wanted to play rock and roll.

I had that experience at school. I went to a Christian school for 6 months in 1981. My music collection was Black Sabbath, Iron Maiden, Thin Lizzy, Rush, AC/DC, Motorhead... I was into heavy metal back then. I also loved bands like the Police, etc. At the school, I was told that this music was of the devil. I wound up smashing all my albums. I felt guilty I was listening to the devil's music. I was only fifteen at the time. So I had that "devil's music" vibe growing up right up through my early twenties. But I didn't care, I was a musician. I wanted to play the guitar. At the time, I wasn't really concerned with the lyrics. I was more concerned about the guitar riffs.

But yeah, we had that kind of energy biting at us all the

time. When we got signed the pastor of the church wanted to be our best friend! All of a sudden, we were the band from his church. That was my first experience with seeing one thing turn into another...just the hypocrisy of it. Now we were the band from his church. Yeah, right, buddy.

Do Christian rock groups have groupies in the traditional sense of the word?
You mean as far as groupies backstage having wild sex? Well, of course that happens. Much of it they do it privately. They hide it from everyone out of a fear of being judged. There was a lot of that going on. Still happens today all throughout the Christian music industry. There's a lot of sex, drugs, and rock and roll, just as much as any secular band. The difference is, the people in the secular industry don't give a shit who knows. They don't really make a big deal about it. They're not in fear of being judged, whereas in the Christian music industry they still do the same shenanigans, but just hide it because if you get found out, there's a good chance you'll lose your livelihood. They don't want the word getting out because it will be, "Ooh look, he's a back-sliding sinner!" But the reality is, we're all in the same boat. We all experience the same struggles.

When did you start to personally question religion?
In 1992 I became interested in learning about the Apollo space missions. I was fascinated by documentaries I saw on TV. I was videotaping documentaries on the Apollo missions. I was so fascinated with how we got to the moon. Then it just went from there... I wanted to learn about the other planets in our solar system. Just watching documentaries on TV, reading

books, etc. It expanded and grew from there. All of a sudden I had a new passion about space and what's out there. It hasn't stopped. I'm a big fan of watching the Science Channel. YouTube came in, all of a sudden you could start watching documentaries from all around the world. It was easy to watch a Neil deGrasse Tyson documentary or a Lawrence Krauss documentary. I was fascinated with these guys. The more documentaries I watched, and the more I read, the more my learnings from the Bible started to fall apart. It just didn't make sense. It took many years of examining what was presented to me on these documentaries. The more I learned, the more I was hard-wiring my brain into that kind of thinking. My old way of thinking started to unwire. It wasn't an overnight thing. I didn't just click and say "I'm an atheist." It took many years to realize I was actually an atheist.

I grew up as a Christian, and I still identified as one up until maybe five years ago, even though I doubted a great many things. The first time I admitted to someone else and myself, for that matter, that I was an atheist, it was a shocking revelation to myself.

It is, because it's a complete change of identity. You're brought up in a mindset. When you're in that mindset you tell yourself, "I'm always gonna believe in God. There's no way I could change. This is who I am." Then all of a sudden, when you do change, it's like a twist on life. It's like a twist on your psyche. It's a challenge because you've lived most of your life thinking that there was a god, now all of a sudden you live in a world where God doesn't exist. You don't believe in God anymore. You really have to dig deep within and think, "Okay, what do I do now? What are my responsibilities? Who am I? Why am I here? What am I doing?" It's a real change. Your identity has completely changed. It's like you're a different person now.

When you came out as an atheist, what were the reactions of your former bandmates?
Well, Peter and I, we're still buddies. We're probably closer now than we've ever been. He knows exactly who I am and what I believe. He knows my heart. He thinks I'm more "Christian" than most Christians. He doesn't care. I've seen his views change as well. We talk a lot. We're going on a motorbike trip in about a month's time. We're gonna be camping out for a couple of weeks and we'll be having a lot of conversations under the stars. He's gonna be telling me where he stands in his beliefs, and he knows exactly where I stand. He knows he doesn't have the power to change my mind. [Laughs.] The power's within. I get to think for myself. I'm not going to give that power away to anyone. But I'm happy to hear your opinions and your viewpoints. We may not agree on them, but I'm happy to hear them. Feel free to express yourself anyway you want. Underneath that, we're both humans, and we both love each other. We're brothers.

The Newsboys appeared in the movie God's Not Dead *a couple of years back. As an atheist, it's a really offensive movie in its portrayal of atheists. Since you're linked to them while also being an atheist, what were your thoughts on that movie?*
I was asked by *The Friendly Atheist* what I thought about the movie so I did a short write-up. I watched the movie with a couple of mates of mine from Australia who've known me most of my life and have seen the whole Newsboys saga from the beginning to now. We watched it together. We all slapped our

foreheads with our palms at exactly the same time. It was just so cliché. They obviously did it because they knew they were going to make a ton of money. The film itself was like a 1986 church play put on film. It was just ridiculous. It's also ridiculous that it made a ton of money. It's an embarrassment to Christianity. It cost two million dollars to make and made over sixty million, so of course they're gonna make a *God's Not Dead 2*. It just wasn't realistic. It demonized everyone else except their own brand of Christianity. That's their whole message. They've been up to these tricks for a long time now. Look, the rest of society is not stupid; we're not going to hear their message and say, "Oh, my goodness, I'm going to abandon everything I've learned about science now and I'm going to follow this!" It's silliness. It plays on vulnerable people's emotions.

How did coming to atheism change your worldview? I mean, as Christians we were taught these things like homosexuals are an abomination. How did it change your perception of the world that went on around you?

I was never against gays anyway. I have gay and lesbian friends, so I never had an issue with that. I have an issue with the church being against it! Being in the church was very confusing. I didn't always agree with them.

When I was a Christian there was a feeling of separation from other religions and atheists. It's that feeling of separation that causes all the problems in the world. People view life through a veil of separation if you don't subscribe to their religion. As a Christian, there's a feeling inside that makes you feel separate from others. But that's just the ego. It's an animalistic way of viewing life. That, to me, is the biggest problem on the planet—that separation to one another. Science tells me that we're all connected, so science has done for me what religion was supposed to do. Through science I now realize that, hey, we're actually all connected. We're all made from elements that were created in supernovas. Now I feel connected with everyone.

As an atheist, I feel it's my responsibility to be the best person I can be, to contribute to the earth and not rape it. When I die, I want to make sure I've contributed to it in a positive way. Without a god judging me. It's our responsibility to leave the planet a better place. You could make the world a better place by smiling more, or by cheering someone up. You could make the world a better place by saying "thank you" more often and by being grateful. Music makes people smile, and I'll continue to do that.

JIM CORNETTE

Jim Cornette is a name that's well known in the world of professional wrestling. Having worked in the field since 1982, Cornette's credentials include the Continental Wrestling Association (CWA), Mid-South Wrestling (MSW), World Championship Wrestling (WCW), and the World Wrestling Federation (WWF, known today as the WWE). Cornette has been a writer, booker, commentator, manager, and wrestler. He's always been known for being a little bit on the obnoxious side, with a brash, in-your-face style that he wears well. Cornette assures us that it's not an act—that this is the real him, and that fact becomes instantly obvious when you listen to his podcast, *The Jim Cornette Experience*.

Beginning in 2009, Cornette began to reveal a political side. He started to speak out against things he saw the right-wing doing that angered him. He also publicly supported President Barack Obama and many Democrats. This progressive attitude and viewpoint is prevalent on his weekly podcast, where he speaks out about his atheism and the things he sees as the dangers of and problems with religion.

I sat down to speak with the often-controversial, always-outspoken Cornette on a variety of topics, ranging from lawmakers who enact policies based on their religion to being an atheist in the world of professional wrestling.

* * *

How does a good ol' boy from Louisville end up being an outspoken, progressive atheist?

It's a long story. I was born a small black child in a log cabin or whatever that thing in the Steve Martin movie is. Basically, I've been an entertainment fan since I was a kid. Not only wrestling, but also movies, radio, music, television. Not only the stars, but the business behind it. I've studied extensively all my life on that because I've applied it to wrestling. I've been in the wrestling bubble. In the Eighties, I was on the road, working 300+ nights a year as a performer. In the Nineties, I ran my own promotion 24 hours a day out of Knoxville, and at the same time worked for WWF and was on the creative team there in Connecticut. And then I came to Louisville and operated the developmental program for WWE and my own promotion, again, 24/7 obsession job. Right? So I was in what they call in wrestling the "wrestling bubble." And I honestly... I wasn't an outspoken atheist, because people look at you so sideways. I wasn't going to go down the streets screaming "There is no God!," right?

But it became applicable to my public persona about 10 or 12 years ago, when I started slacking off on my wrestling pursuits. I worked TNA part-time. But, you know, trying to get off the road, etc... At the same time comes 9/11. Two wars. The global financial crisis. And I start losing money and reading in the papers about what the fuck we're doing and realize George Bush is an idiot. And then when I started paying attention to that and politics, started paying attention to the fact that—this is what enrages me—this is where these worlds have collided. We have, among all the other problems and all the other issues we have as a country and as a planet, we have, still in this day and age, in the 21st century, people being elected to public office to form laws, make public policy, and influence our entire lives, from where we live, to how much money we have or don't have, to what we eat, etc., based on what a supernatural, fictitious, supreme being would approve of! I find that unacceptable. Because the saying is that you're allowed in a free society to believe anything you want to believe personally, but in this instance, people's religious beliefs are being forced onto me and form, in part, my life and what I'm able to do. It's ludicrous!

That's where my two interests of bashing conservative politicians and bashing religion have converged and come into play, and now that I do the podcast, I'm more outspoken about it. Because before, when I was speaking in wrestling, it was within the context of the program, whether I was announcing a wrestling match or working as a performer on the show. But now I'm myself in not only my public appearances but the shows that I do. I can't stop talking about this because it makes my head explode.

I understand that. It seems like it's getting worse every day.

If you look, almost every society, as they become more educated and more enlightened, becomes less religious or dependent on religion, or strictly dogmatic about it, or whatever. This whole thing converges. The evangelicals are a huge contingent of the Donald Trump supporters. That means that these godly religious people will accept the most immoral, unethical, untruthful things—basically the antithesis of anything that they say that a godly, religious person should be, in the White House, if it will make sure that they get conservative judges that will make church mandatory and destroy women's rights of whether she has a baby or not. They're willing to cross that bridge and have this complete pig in the White House if it furthers their own agenda. That's why I said they're not about morals and principles; they're about *their* morals and principles. And they're fanatics! Because it's come down to the point where the majority of Americans are certainly not Trump supporters but they're still religious. But the most religious people are the people who take this stuff the most seriously, because, as you know, religion, in large part, lends itself to fanatics and extremists. Just like other people with mental health issues flock to something that they can be fanatical or extreme about. Basically, that loud, vocal minority of people who really take this shit seriously and will stop at nothing to achieve their aims are the basis of the Republican party. [Laughs.]

You talked about the Trump followers being religious. I've kind of had this theory for awhile... I think spending your entire life believing in something that's probably bullshit kind of leads you to a path of being susceptible to believing the kind of shit Donald Trump is selling. Even though it should be obvious, they become trained to believe whatever they hear.

I have a comparison, or a simile if you will, that I use on my show. It's amazing that two people can walk side-by-side down the street and I can look down at my feet on the sidewalk and see this huge pile of dog shit, and say, "Holy shit! Don't step in that dog shit!" and the guy next to me can say, "No, that's a tasty cheeseburger!" "You're crazy, that's a pile of dog shit!" "No, look, it's a tasty cheeseburger!" And they'll pick it up and eat it to prove it's a tasty cheeseburger! But normal folks are looking at a pile of dog shit. I don't know how something like this can be solved. Because they say if you call Trump supporters stupid, or if you call the very religious stupid, it'll make them mad. You can't reach them that way. They'll just always think that way. At this point, if they haven't been reached by now, they're not reachable.

But more to your topic... I was a fan of George Carlin, and I saw him several times live. I got all the DVDs. Bill Maher is the closest thing now. But most comedians now, and over the past 10 or 20 years, the really hot, edgy comedians have been able to point out the ridiculousness of almost every backstory of almost every religion, right? And they get huge crowds of people who are laughing. And I'm just wondering, has that made the really religious more like, "I'll show you!" You can't not laugh when you break it down. People are still sitting there going, "No, it's a tasty cheeseburger!" You can't help but laugh at those people. Somebody said over here on Twitter the other day, "It's a free society, you have a right to your beliefs, you have a right to express them, and I have a right to laugh at them if they're really fucking stupid". Once again, I don't understand it. I don't know if you've seen my website, but have you read the commentaries section?

I say religion is cosmetic surgery for the soul.

I was going to ask you about that one, but yeah, I read that. It was great.

I can understand if you're in a foxhole. Or if you're in death row or in prison. Or if you're fatally ill, knock on wood. Okay, you might be more inclined to go, "let's go with this," but I just don't understand the people like the Mike Pences of the world. They walk around with that smug little look on their faces. The Jerry Falwell smirk. Like they know something you don't know and they're trying to bring you along because you're such a little simpleton. They're pedaling fantasy and fiction to gullible people and people who need to hear that. Here's the thing, and I guess it's a step up... A lot of wrestlers go to rehab, and I find that most people, wrestlers or otherwise, when they come out of rehab, they've exchanged the one addiction for another. Now it's, "God will show me the way!" You've exchanged the substance abuse problem for a mental issue that you have to keep straight. Believe in the obvious bullshit. That if you just sat down for a minute... The Easter Bunny story is probably not as far fetched as some of the backstory of some major religions that billions of people around the world follow. And once again, that's fairly related to religion. The origination of Easter. Jesus rose from the dead and put eggs underneath the children's pillows? I don't know. The bunnies don't lay eggs. I don't know how that whole thing worked out! [Laughs.] It's very frustrating.

You spent a lot of years working in the world of professional wrestling. I don't know this as a fact, but that strikes me as an environment that isn't probably particularly conducive to atheism. I'm sure you didn't go around and spouting this stuff, but what was it like being in that environment?

Well, actually, in the Eighties, when I was primarily in the locker rooms with the boys, there was not that much talk about politics or religion. It was the matches, the ribs, the girls, the other territories, the house, the business. It was just the guys, right? But then, fast forward. Once again, there were always some guys that we used to laugh at. I don't want to mention his name, but there was one guy who was one of the underneath guys. Everybody liked him and he was a good talented wrestler, but he started leaving pamphlets saying "Jesus saves." He'd leave 'em in the bathroom. He'd go in all the stalls and leave 'em sitting on the toilet paper thing because he didn't want to come out and give them to you personally until he knew you, but he was trying to spread the word. [Laughs.] And we laughed. Me and the boys would go, "Oh, he's spreading God again!"

And then, fast forward to TNA, I think around 2007. Me and Dutch Mantell are producers of the show for the various matches, promo segments, etc. Dutch is on the creative team. And we are running around, trying to find all the talent, the guys in the main event. The guys in the world title match. You start getting things together and organized, and this was a Sunday, right? But they had organized this special prayer session for all the believers upstairs in one of the buildings. I'm like, "Jesus fucking Christ! They could've gone to church this morning." It's 2:30 in the afternoon on pay-per-view day and we can't find the champions, you know? It's just, it was... [Sighs.]

Anyway, so things change. But then again, there's no official talk of religion from the WWE because they got people that sit down and check off when all the key diversities of the talent are on the program. If they started getting into mentioning religion, they'd have to mention every religion, and they wouldn't have time for it. But no, you know, it wasn't a big deal in the locker rooms. Nobody was sitting there talking about it... I mean, Ric Flair's favorite line is "God bless you and your family," you know? But it's not like he was saying, "Okay, let us open the book and pray before our match," you know? So it's not like it came to any arguments that I ever saw.

What kind of feedback have you gotten from wrestling fans now that you've become more outspoken about these kinds of things?

For the people who like that kind of thing, it's the kind of thing those people like. The people who like what I say, love it because I just don't give a shit. That's my gimmick. I tell the truth. But then I'll get emails, or I'll get tweets from people saying, "Well, I used to have respect for you, but I can't believe you mock my faith!" or "I used to have respect for you but I can't believe you're one of those libtards!" I think if the people who use the right-wing buzzwords—that Alex Jones type shit, like cucks and libtards—don't like me, then I'm happy. I'm doing something right. Because I don't want them to like me.

And if the people who I'm not... I'm sorry, but if some people think I'm mocking their faith, I'm mocking their faith! What if I came out and said, "You know, that moon is so delicious! It's green cheese! And, as a matter of fact, I'm going to introduce a bill to my local government that we should have Green Cheese Day on the moon. And everybody goes out and has some green cheese and honor the..." What the? It's just ridiculous! So as long as they're trying to have Supreme Court justices overturn laws that a woman can choose whether she has a baby or not because God says so, I've got to be against that. And because most of the evangelical conservatives are also the ones who think that all these children getting shot in school would be safer if a bunch more people had a bunch more guns! That's fucking ridiculous! So I've gotta say something about that, too! And I point out how ridiculous and stupid and nonsensical some of these things are and it hits a nerve, and they don't like it. And I don't care.

It's interesting how many bad ideas there are out there right now, and how they're all basically coming from the same people? The guns thing, you know? All the conservative shit. All of the religious shit. It's always the same usual suspects. It drives you crazy.

Yes. And you know what? All of the people that listen to my podcast, and I encourage more people to do so, they tell me they're tired of having everybody on the right on talk radio. I mean, Rush Limbaugh now looks like he ought to be on NPR. Because the right is so much more over the top now than it used to be. Twitter, Alex Jones, and the fucking people on Fox News. And how did they get the same blonde that's got twelve different names on Fox News? [Laughs.] Isn't that wild? But all those people are always mad. They're yelling. They're upset, and they're calling people to action and rousing the rabble.

And the people on the left, who are apparently sane and reasonable people, don't have that shit and that's why all the people on the right get stirred up and mad enough to go vote. And the people on the left are like, "Oh, it'll be okay." So I'm the guy on the left going "No! The ship is sinking unless you start bailing, so get out there, motherfucker, and run these people out of town!" That's my nature. Whether it be wrestling promos or whatever, this is not a gimmick. As people who know me well will tell you, I can cut a promo on a ham sandwich if it pisses me off. What the hell, mustard instead of mayo? What the! You know. But somebody needs to stir people up and say, "Hey, look, normal, sane people, whether you believe in God or not, you don't want your kids shot at school. It's obvious from what we're seeing in front of our face that the President of the United States is a lying douchebag real estate fraud, so we need to rectify that and get some Democrats because the Republicans have no balls."

It's nice to know now that the Pope himself is especially against grown adult priests diddling little boys. It's good that we know that now, because they do it so often. If you're Catholic and you find out over and over that in repeated instances, over periods of decades, in places all around the world, that Catholic priests have indeed been, and admitted to, and convicted of, and apologized for, molesting a small child, small children, why do you want to take your kids there? I don't understand that. Here's the thing: it's because its religion's supposed to be sacred and not supposed to be touched. But if it was AMC Cinemas... Got one in every town, right? Kids love to go to movies. Tons of kids go to movies. How long would it take if just one of the AMC Cinemas was convicted of hiding pedophiles as their ticket takers and ushers for them to go out of business? It would be a ghost town! But because it's religion this happens over and over and over. Then you have the unfortunate convergence in the United States where guns practically are the religion, in some cases. They go hand in hand. They're more fixated on their guns... As a matter of fact, the famous line which popped me and I immediately loved this man for life: "They cling to their guns and their religion because they're scared, because they don't know what the fuck to do because the world is changing." And truer words have never been spoken.

And that was supposed to be the really offensive thing that Obama said. But Trump says shit fifty times worse every day of the week and that's acceptable. And they'll do that whataboutism thing where they go, "well when Obama did this," and they're never comparable. Or applicable, really. And the thing that drives me crazy is Obama was a guy they were mad at for liking spicy mustard and wearing a tan suit. And Trump, every day, goes five million times beyond any of those infractions, and they're cool with it. They don't see. They're still like, "Well, that fucking Hillary," or "That fucking Obama."

And her emails! And her emails! I think they're nuts. And that's the thing. What we have to do, and the broader picture in the short term, just to get this under control so some kind of sanity can return and prevail, is everybody needs to get out and vote as many Republicans out of office as possible because they're all either complicit or bat shit crazy. They're either complicit because they know all this shit's bullshit but they're doing it for the power, or they're bat shit crazy because they don't know all this shit is bat shit crazy. So either way, they need to move over or they'll fuck everything up.

I just wish I could say I would live to see the day, but it's going to be, unfortunately, longer than that, when people evolve out of religion. And yes, we can understand that happening in primitive times, when leeches were the cutting edge medical technology, right? I can understand that. And I can understand the Native American tribes and ancient civilizations around the world. The sky creature. The giver of life. That whole thing. But now that we know kind of enough of what's going on to realize that we're in charge of our whole destiny... That was always the whole thing. They couldn't control people back then because there was no organized law and order. They had to tell somebody something, "You're a bad person, and you're going to burn in hell forever more! So try to be good. We can't stop you right now." And give them a reward. "But if you're good, you go to heaven, you see all your friends, family, shit on the clouds!"

Okay, that obviously isn't going to work in this day and age as a control factor for most people. And also, I always think you're either good or you're not, regardless of what you believe. And eventually, we will evolve out of this and realize we're running this shit. God's not gonna save the planet, and we have to, instead of poisoning the atmosphere. "Well, God created a flood!" Or whatever. We're running this shit, we're in charge of ourselves, we have to find our way to the fucking picnic 'cause there's no GPS. But as long as people have the crack chips, they think, "Well, we can pray to..." They're not going to take matters into their own hands! And also, it's just ludicrous for people who have half a lick of common sense! It's just frustrating.

I'm not against all the good things that churches do on a local basis, but why does it have to be about praying to an invisible god to have a local community group that gets together, is building, and raises money for sick kids' medical treatment or money for food for the hungry or whatever. It's not a law that the only way you can have that kind of gathering is if you pray to a fictitious supreme being at the same time. If we could ever get to the point where we evolve out of the ridiculous part of religion and get people to all get together and be nice to each other... Wouldn't that be nice? Wouldn't that be great? Imagine! [Laughs.]

CHRIS ROY

Chris Roy was born and raised in South Mississippi. Having no sufficient male role model to speak of, he ran wild and committed a criminal act or twelve. As his bio explains, Roy was "roaming the towns and wilds of the rich and poor, thieving and thinking without a curfew." Like most teenagers, he thought he had all the answers. Then in 1999, at the age of 18, he learned otherwise. As he discusses in this interview, Roy got into a bloody brawl that left his opponent dead. Making matters worse, Roy tried to cover up what he'd done, hiding the body. He ultimately got caught. The following year, he was sentenced to life in prison. Like many people sentenced to prison, he continued with his life of crime even after he was behind bars.

In 2007, that changed. By this time Roy had read countless novels in prison and had begun writing both fiction and nonfiction. He began to take writing seriously. He stopped committing crimes, instead putting pen to pad and writing about them. He has since written a number of crime novels and novellas.

His most recent work is the short story collection *Her Name Is Mercie*.

Roy is also an atheist. Given his somewhat unique circumstances, I thought it might be interesting to sit down and talk to him about doing a lifetime bid, his writing career, and his views on religion.

* * *

What kind of environment did you grow up in? Was it a religious environment?

My mother and father were not religious. My grandparents were. Most of my family attended church. My mom even sent my brother and I off to Bible Camp during summer a few times. I was exposed to that, so it wasn't like I was raised in an atheist home or had no religion in my life whatsoever. It was an interesting childhood, we had a happy childhood actually. We didn't have much. We grew up in a trailer. We weren't starving or anything, but I knew what it was like to wear K-Mart specials while the other kids were riding chrome bicycles and wearing name brand clothes. I got into stealing things at an early age, got into a lot of trouble, and so I was exposed to religion in the juvenile detention center. I've been around it, and I've done studies on it.

At what point did you come to realize you didn't believe in God?

When I was in high school I started discovering things in biology and geology. I'm probably going to sound like a hippie when I say this, but I had my first epiphany about this when I was on LSD and then later on mushrooms. It takes away your ego, which is a big part of religion, I believe. I had some experiences with nature when I was hallucinating and after those experiences, I wanted to know more, so I actually started paying attention more in Biology and Geology. I started paying attention to nature around me, and thinking about what that all meant in relation to the Bible and other things I was taught growing up—what I had been taught at Bible Camp. My grandma used to say the devil was in me, and it just became ridiculous that people would say things like that. It didn't matter. I didn't believe in the old man in the clouds.

So, the philosophy of it... I have respect for that; for pretty much any religion, the philosophy of it. If somebody were to follow that and actually live that lifestyle, then they can be productive and progress, and, to be very real, stay out of trouble. But I don't believe the magical thinking part of it.

You got into trouble and ended up being incarcerated when you were 18. What happened? Would you like to talk a little bit about that?

Sure. Let me give you some more background about myself first. When I was a teenager I worked full-time during summers at my uncle's junkyards. Later on, I got a job working at a transmission shop. My mom kicked me out for selling drugs, so I had my own place. I went back to school. I had to repeat 12th grade because I had missed too many days. I was out selling drugs and throwing parties, that sort of thing. I had good grades, in 11th and 12th grade, anyways. But that was my life. It was more about money and friends. I didn't have any strong male figures in my life. My father wasn't around, I didn't have anybody I really looked up to and respected to follow and keep me out of trouble. So I was doing my own thing and heading in my own direction, and I had a plan. I didn't plan on selling drugs forever. I wanted to go to mechanic school in Nashville. I had the opportunity to. I just made some poor decisions.

One night I was drinking, working on a car with a buddy of mine. It was a school night, actually. The guy I had a disagreement with, he was a Vietnamese gang leader and drug dealer. He was also 18. I was 18, and my friend there was 19. It was the three of us, we're all teenagers. I had been working for this guy for a while, selling drugs; cocaine, ecstasy, and marijuana. We had a disagreement over money. It's a long story. The disagreement went on for a few months, and it escalated into him threatening my friend and then threatening me. We were going to clash and so it was just a chance meeting at my friend's house. He came at me with very aggressive words, and when he and his guys came like that, it was for business; he didn't play around. He and his crew were known for drive-bys, that sort of thing.

My first thought was to beat his ass before he could pull out a weapon. So when he came at me aggressively, I jumped on him and we were fighting. It was just fist fighting, there weren't any weapons, but he ended up dying from his injuries. His neck was damaged. He suffocated. So here we are, my friend and I, looking down at the body, and we were scared to death. His parents were home. Did they hear it? Do we call the police? No, that's a bad idea, then we'll go to prison forever. Okay, you do what you do. If the guy's gang finds out, they're going to come after us, they're going to kill us.

So we covered it up. In that state of mind, you're a teenager, you're not thinking rationally to begin with, and you're sure enough not thinking rationally now... You just killed someone. Someone's dead right here. It was just one bad decision after another. We took the body out in the middle of nowhere and buried him. We put the car in the river.

Four months later, they arrested us. It was a long investigation. They didn't know who did it. They finally made their way around to us, and my friend told them everything. He testified against me. He took a manslaughter deal and testified against me. I had a public defender at trial, and that didn't work well for me. Nobody had money. The people that have money, they get off. I've seen a lot of cases similar to mine that were dropped down to manslaughter and guys were getting 8 years, 12 years, whatever. They took me to trial on capital murder and tried to say that we robbed the guy and killed him, but they couldn't prove the robbery. That was ridiculous. But they did convict me of murder. I'm sentenced, under law, to be given parole eligibility when I'm 65 years old.

The stereotype is that when most people go to prison, they find religion. That hasn't been the case for you. Would you like to talk about that?

A lot of people go to prison, or they go to jail, and they find God. When I was in the county jail, they had church service every week and the guys could go out of the cell block, down the hall to a holding tank, and pile up in there. They had a preacher come in there and he would talk for a bit, and everybody would pray. I went to it a few times, really just to get out of the cell block. It was crowded, guys sleeping all over the floor everywhere. The cell blocks were for 8 people and there are 23 people piled up in there. It was a hard time, actually.

I like to experience different things. I don't limit myself on what I read or what I watch or listen to, so I like to check out the views of different types of people. I went and checked out the Christian viewpoint, even at that age. It was the same thing. There was just something so ridiculous about this and I just couldn't understand why people didn't see that. There's nothing rational about this. They go on and on about all these people in the Bible and what they did in these stories, but they're just myths and legends.

It was actually about that time that I started realizing how myths and legends came about. Back in a time when these people lived, they'd do something that was incredible that spread like wildfire, and became a legend so quickly, it ended up being a myth. I used to talk to people about that in the county jail and have long discussions into the night about different topics like that. I remember a conversation I brought up to religious guys, you know, just to hear their views on it, and I asked them, "How do you think these stories came about?" And they quoted the Bible, they were just so indoctrinated with this. It'd always come back to faith. It was really dependent on that one concept. I would talk to them and say, give me an example. Say you are a warrior in Scotland or something. You had a battle and killed a bunch of guys and saved your buddy. That's a great story. Your clan there is going to be very proud of you, you're a hero, there's going to be songs sung about you. It's going to be spread around. And by the time your story reaches England, you're seven feet tall and have killed 20 Englishmen! That story gets written down. It gets made into song and passed on for generations, in the books, and you become a legend, or even a myth. I can give several examples like that. And the Bible is no different.

I had this understanding of things and then I was just absorbing everything I could about science, and from good quality sources, too. I would question older people who had studied religion for most of their life about the stories of the Bible, and the timelines. Some people believe the earth is 6,000 years old. I wanted to know things about that. You know, *why* do you believe that? Because a book tells you that? A book that has been revised countless times by many men, who have their own focus and agendas? There were no real, solid answers.

When you have religious conversations with other prisoners, how are your views usually met? Do people get angry? How does that go?

Every other week or so we have these church groups that come around. They're just volunteers. They're older men. One of them is a biker group. They're pretty cool. Some of them come around, and if you tell them, "Hey, I'm an atheist, I'm not really interested in talking about God," they'll talk about it even more. They're cool, they'll talk about it, but they won't force a prayer on you. I try to be polite. I'm never rude about this sort of thing, but I will tell them I'm an atheist and I'm not really interested in talking about that.

Some days, I just say, "Thank you, give me the daily bread" and move along. Some of them will stop and want to ask what happened to me, what's wrong with me, like there's something wrong with me for being an atheist. I don't get hostile or anything, but I will put them on the spot about their beliefs.

Sometimes they actually get angry. One time a guy got mad and started getting loud, saying that I think I'm a god. "You think you're a god!" I was like, "What're you talking about?" He was being completely irrational about it. An officer had to come and calm him down. He'd say things like, "If you die, where would you go today?" And I would say, "Well, I was dead for billions of years before I was alive and it wasn't a problem then," and they really don't have a response for that.

They'll ask me things about Darwin. Darwin, the thing about him converting to Christianity before he died. I tell them that was likely written by a Christian in a time where people who went against Christianity would lose their heads, literally, so it was just a different time when that story came about.

You've become a published crime author since you've been imprisoned. How did that come about?

It was about eleven years ago now. In 2007 I started writing my first short stories. I was on high-risk with several guys also on high-risk. We were all escape risks. I had escaped twice. Several others were aspiring writers. A friend of mine, Roy Harper, was writing a series that ended up being a two book series. I read the handwritten manuscript and I was very inspired by that. Another buddy of mine, he had some books on writing. Things like *How To Write A Novel*. I was getting into that, and I wanted to start a website with my friend that would have essays we'd write on how to commit crimes and get away with them. It was weird, because we were doing that and we were also writing things for kids, teenagers especially, on different ways to hustle that's not illegal. There are different hustles out there kids can do that aren't illegal; keeps them out of trouble. We were on both sides of the wall. The website was not a success. I think we got a few essays posted on a MySpace blog. I had written some short stories that were basically how-to manuals on how to steal cars and flip them, how to do identity theft, ATM scams, different scams on Craigslist, how to cook meth.

A lot of these crimes, I learned while in prison. Prison is a finishing school for criminals, basically. It's not a correctional institutional like they say. I came here and learned all these different crimes from all these different people who are very experienced criminals, and thought, wow, I've seen some amazing things. So I created my own stories. I created these two characters that were criminals, and they would do these crimes, these scams, and they were hilarious. They were fun. They were brilliant. They were dangerous. I didn't know anything about writing at that time. At that point, I had read hundreds of novels and had written a thousand letters and dog-eared a few dictionaries. I had enough writing ability, and my vocabulary was at the point where I could sit down and write something that was decent.

The people that read the original handwritten short stories liked them. Prisoners with very long sentences, high risk, a couple people on death row, and all of them were long time convicts who had read numerous books. They knew a good book, and they weren't afraid to tell me if it was shit. But they were telling me it was good. So I took it seriously and started studying the craft of fiction writing. My next project was more involved. It took a little over a year to finish, and ended up becoming a trilogy. It was 700-and-something pages, handwritten. I wrote four handwritten drafts. I had this big mountain of paper after a year, and a friend of mine typed it up, and I ended up typing the rest of it on my phone. We self-published. That didn't work out too well. Now it's published as a trilogy by New Pulp Press called *Shocking Circumstances*.

Then I immediately started another project, *Sharp as a Razor*, which was just as long in length and took 16 months to finish. It ended up being a trilogy, as well, and New Pulp Press published that. I just came out with a short story collection called *Her Name Is Mercie*. It's been a while since I wrote anything, because I wanted to go back and hit the books, and change my style of writing. Tom Vater was my mentor. He gave me a lot of great advice, and has been working with me the last few years on writing. He took a look at *Shocking Circumstances* and didn't like it. He told me a bunch of different things I needed to do to change my style and how to repackage it, and to start practicing with short stories. He told me what to read, what I need to look at, that sort of thing. So over time, my style changed and I started writing short stories, and now I have a collection of them.

What does the future look like for you at the moment?

The law that I'm sentenced under is actually unconstitutional. A guy in Mississippi that was sentenced to life before 1995, they're eligible for parole after 10 years. If they're sentenced to life after 2014, they're eligible for parole after 10 years. The 19 year period in between, they're eligible after they turn 65 years old, no matter how old they are. So a guy that's 18 years old, like I was, has to do 47 years. A guy that's 50 has to do 15 years. It doesn't make any sense.

There are House bills coming up just about every year that could change the law and make it retroactive so that those guys in the 19-year period get parole after 10 years. But they're not passing them. What would happen if they did pass them is they'd be forced to parole hundreds of guys that have murders or robberies, and they don't want to do that. It's going to make them look bad. They're getting away with it, and they're figuring out how to make money off it.

In my opinion, the parole laws should be a lot different. If a person goes to prison for drugs, violence, whatever, and after 10 years, you look at their record and there's none of that whatsoever...no drugs, no violence, then they should be given a second chance. If you look at the record, and that behavior has continued, either the institution isn't doing their job or the guy isn't going to be rehabilitated. I'm speaking for people convicted of murder, really. I think that the parole laws should be like this. If you're 18 years old, then the maximum you have to spend for life in prison is 18 years. Eligible at 10. If you're 40 years old, your max should be 40 years. Eligible at 10. You shouldn't be given more time because you're younger, you shouldn't be given less time because you're older. If you're older, then hey, you know better. You've had time to develop and you're unlikely to be rehabilitated. If you're 30, 40 years old, and you commit a murder, well, then your max time should be 30 or 40 years. Eligible at 10. They're throwing young people away and they're letting older people go earlier. It's backwards. A lot of it comes down to there's too much religion in the court here, and there needs to be more brains in it.

Andrew J. Rausch is a a freelance film journalist, author, and celebrity interviewer. He has published more than twenty books on the subject of popular culture, including *The Films of Martin Scorsese and Robert De Niro*, *Making Movies with Orson Welles* (with Gary Graver), and *The Cinematic Misadventures of Ed Wood* (with Charles E. Pratt, Jr.). His work has appeared in *Shock Cinema*, both *Screem* and *Scream* magazines, *Senses of Cinema*, *Diabolique*, *Creative Screenwriting*, *Cemetery Dance*, *Film Threat*, *Bright Lights Film Journal*, and *Images: A Journal of Film and Popular Culture*. He has written several works of fiction including *Mad World*, *Elvis Presley: CIA Assassin*, *Riding Shotgun and Other American Cruelties*, and the short story collection *Death Rattles*. He has also worked as a screenwriter, producer, and actor on numerous straight-to-video horror films.

ALSO BY CLASH BOOKS

TRAGEDY QUEENS: STORIES INSPIRED BY LANA DEL REY & SYLVIA PLATH
Edited by Leza Cantoral

GIRL LIKE A BOMB
Autumn Christian

THIS BOOK IS BROUGHT TO YOU BY MY STUDENT LOANS
Megan J. Kaleita

NEW VERONIA
M.S. Coe

DARK MOONS RISING IN A STARLESS NIGHT
Mame Bougouma Diene

NOHO GLOAMING & THE CURIOUS CODA OF ANTHONY SANTOS
Daniel Knauf (Creator of HBO's Carnivàle)

99 POEMS TO CURE WHATEVER'S WRONG WITH YOU OR CREATE THE PROBLEMS YOU NEED
Sam Pink

FOGHORN LEGHORN

Big Bruiser Dope Boy

IF YOU DIED TOMORROW I WOULD EAT YOUR CORPSE

Wrath James White

THE ANARCHIST KOSHER COOKBOOK

Maxwell Bauman

HORROR FILM POEMS

Christoph Paul

NIGHTMARES IN ECTASY

Brendan Vidito

THE VERY INEFFECTIVE HAUNTED HOUSE

Jeff Burk

ZOMBIE PUNKS FUCK OFF

Edited by Sam Richard

THIS BOOK AIN'T NUTTIN TO FUCK WITH: A WU-TANG TRIBUTE ANTHOLOGY

Edited by Christoph Paul & Grant Wamack

WALK HAND IN HAND INTO EXTINCTION - STORIES INSPIRED BY TRUE DETECTIVE

Edited by Christoph Paul & Leza Cantoral

WE PUT THE LIT IN LITERARY

CLASHBOOKS.COM

yesclash.com

Twitter, IG,Facebook @CLASHBooks

Email: clashmediabooks@gmail.com

www.ingramcontent.com/pod-product-compliance
Lightning Source LLC
Chambersburg PA
CBHW030108100526
44591CB00009B/334